ABOLITIONISTS

of

SOUTH CENTRAL PENNSYLVANIA

ABOLITIONISTS

of

SOUTH CENTRAL PENNSYLVANIA

COOPER H. WINGERT

THE
History
PRESS

Published by The History Press
Charleston, SC
www.historypress.com

First published 2018

Manufactured in the United States

ISBN 9781467139144

Library of Congress Control Number: 2018945797

CONTENTS

CONTENTS

NOTE TO READERS

This book is organized on a county-by-county basis. Larger themes, such as the influence of Benjamin Lundy, William Lloyd Garrison and other leading abolitionists, recur throughout the chapters. Chapters 2 through 6 are organized this way, introducing the reader to local personalities, the social climates of their respective counties and the national figures who influenced them. Chapters 7 through 9 are more topically constructed, centered on political issues, such as the Fugitive Slave Law and John Brown's Raid, and local responses. (Similarly, the prologue and chapter 1 touch on the roots of abolitionism in America and are more topical than geographical.) This book is oriented as a history of abolitionism in South Central Pennsylvania, set against the backdrop of national events.

The precise workings of the Underground Railroad are covered in my previous book, *Slavery and the Underground Railroad in South Central Pennsylvania*. In that book, I discussed the history of slavery and slaveholding in Pennsylvania dating back to colonial times, as well as the development and work of the Underground Railroad leading up to the Civil War. By contrast, this book is a history of ideas and the people who embraced and championed them. It is an attempt to give more attention to local abolitionists themselves, focusing on the ideas, values and convictions that prompted these otherwise unassuming men and women to take dangerous stances, risking their lives, property and freedom to do what they believed was right.

ACKNOWLEDGEMENTS

In the process of researching, writing and editing this manuscript, I am indebted to many people. They include my ever-supportive family, as well as Craig and Sharon Caba, Ann Hull, Stephen Kohler, Walter Meshaka, Scott Mingus Sr., James Schmick, Janet Taylor, Austin Willi and—invariably—the staffs of the numerous libraries, archives and repositories I visited while researching. Particular thanks go to John Grayshaw, Barbara Scull and John Ziats of Middletown, who directed my attention to the town's often-overlooked African American community at Five Points. Without their collective encouragement and insights, this project would not have been possible.

"WE HAVE THE WOLF BY THE EAR"

SLAVERY IN AMERICA

T o Thomas Jefferson, it had always been a foregone conclusion that slavery's very existence caused "an unhappy influence on the manners of our people." The "whole commerce between master and slave is a perpetual exercise of the most boisterous passions," he contemplated amid the din of the American Revolution. Slavery, the Virginia planter declared, embodied

> the most unremitting despotism on the one part, and degrading submissions on the other. Our children see this, and learn to imitate it; for man is an imitative animal. This quality is the germ of all education in him. From his cradle to his grave he is learning to do what he sees others do....The parent storms, the child looks on, catches the lineaments of wrath, puts on the same airs in the circle of smaller slaves, gives a loose to the worst of passions, and thus nursed, educated, and daily exercised in tyranny, cannot but be stamped by it with odious peculiarities.

At the age of thirty-two, Jefferson readily acknowledged the hypocrisy of a slaveholding nation dedicated to his own proposition that "all men are created equal." He struggled to grapple with the reality that permitted "one half [of] the citizens...to trample on the rights of the other." Fearing a potential slave revolt, he wrote: "I tremble for my country when I reflect that

God is just: that his justice cannot sleep for ever: that considering numbers, nature and natural means only, a revolution of the wheel of fortune, an exchange of situation is among possible events."[1]

When he drafted the Declaration of Independence in 1776, the Virginia slaveholder laid the blame at the feet of King George. Jefferson wrote:

> *He has waged cruel war against human nature itself, violating its most sacred rights of life and liberty in the persons of a distant people who never offended him, captivating & carrying them into slavery in another hemisphere, or to incur miserable death in their transportation thither…. Determined to keep open a market where MEN should be bought & sold, he has prostituted his negative for suppressing every legislative attempt to prohibit or to restrain this execrable commerce.*

In a foreshadowing of what was to come, this paragraph was struck out from the document to appease delegates from South Carolina and Georgia. These fellow southerners, Jefferson sighed remissively, "had never attempted to restrain the importation of slaves, and who on the contrary still wished to continue it." Even an assortment of northerners, he later recalled, "felt a little tender under those censures," Jefferson perceived, "for tho' their people have very few slaves themselves yet they had been pretty considerable carriers of them to others."[2]

Jefferson resigned himself, reflecting several decades later

> *that the public mind would not yet bear the proposition, nor will it bear it even at this day…. Yet the day is not distant when it must bear and adopt it, or worse will follow. Nothing is more certainly written in the book of fate than that these people are free. Nor is it less certain that two races, equally free, cannot live in the same government. Nature, habit, opinion has drawn indelible lines of distinction between them. It is still in our power to direct the process of emancipation and deportation peaceably and in such slow degree as that the evil will wear off insensibly, and their place be…filled by white laborers. If on the contrary it is left to force itself on, human nature must shudder at the prospect held up.*[3]

By the early 1800s, reluctant reformers such as Jefferson hesitated. Slavery, by all means an evil, was a task to be left to the next generation. With the abolition of the transatlantic slave trade in 1808, they believed that slavery would die out on its own, perhaps helped along by a pragmatic approach to be enacted by their sons and grandsons. However, this future inexorably changed with the Louisiana Purchase in 1803, doubling the size of the young nation and opening up millions of new acreage throughout the fertile Mississippi Valley. To distribute this land, the federal government created the General Land Office in 1812.

However, the checks and balances that had been put in place to distribute modest tracts of land to ordinary citizens were quickly overwhelmed. Wealthy slaveholders, anxious to accumulate additional lands in the new territories, soon found loopholes.[4] "It is…a fact," complained one Land Office registrar, "that many of the very wealthy inhabitants, send overseers & slaves, or hire men to make improvements on the most choice places."[5] When the Land Office held public auctions to sell tracts, wealthy planters often colluded beforehand, agreeing not to out-bid one another.

These practices were all much to the dismay of working-class whites throughout the South, who watched countless tracts of land slip out of their reach. "We presume," sneered a disgusted Alabama newspaper, "that the gentlemen speculators formed their plans on the commonly received principle, that the public is a goose, and that while its enchanting plumage offered so many temptations to pluck a few feathers, no other danger was to be apprehended than that of being hissed at!"[6]

With new acreage opening up, the economic might of slavery moved inland. In South Carolina alone, an estimated 83,000 slaves were moved westward each year, amounting to an annual loss of $500,000 in capital. In 1820, Alabama was home to 41,879 enslaved African Americans. In just ten years, that number more than doubled, to some 117,000 slaves. In the same period, Mississippi's enslaved population went from 32,000 to 65,000 and Louisiana's from nearly 70,000 to 110,000. More than economic power, the expansion of slavery represented the cultivation of an identity that intertwined the idea of being "southern" with the existence of slavery. A threat to slavery was now, more than ever before, a threat to the South itself.[7]

In many coastal and tidewater areas, enslaved populations far outnumbered their white counterparts. Fears of bloody revolts stifled talk about the morality of slavery. In the global Age of Revolution and Enlightenment, slavery's very presence was nothing less than a ticking time bomb. Jefferson himself entertained apocalyptic nightmares for the future for American slavery. "We have the wolf by the ear," he wrote in 1820, "and we can neither hold him, nor safely let him go." The Virginian warned that the "revolutionary storm, now sweeping the globe, will be upon us, and happy if we make timely provision to give it an easy passage over our land.…If something is not done, & soon done, we shall be the murderers of our own children." He spoke for many southerners when he declared, "The day which begins our combustion must be near at hand; and only a single spark is wanting to make that day to-morrow."[8]

By the 1820s, slavery had become an increasingly sensitive issue. Before, many southern politicians had openly admitted their qualms with the "peculiar institution." In 1816, South Carolina's John Calhoun—later known as a zealous pro-slavery theorist—apologized for his state's role in continuing the African slave trade. In a speech delivered on the floor of the House of Representatives, Calhoun told colleagues that he "felt ashamed of such a tolerance, and took a large part of the disgrace," as he represented "a part of the Union, by whose influence it might be supposed to have been introduced."[9] However, with bloody slave revolts reverberating throughout the Atlantic world—most famously Nat Turner's 1831 rebellion in Virginia—slave owners grew more reluctant to criticize the institution that had shaped their world.

IN EARLY NINETEENTH-CENTURY AMERICA, who opposed slavery? Although many, including Jefferson, had lamented bondage in the abstract, who was working actively to end slavery? In reality, the seeds of what became known as abolitionism were sown long before the nineteenth century, by men and women who would not be alive to see their work come to fruition.

Pennsylvania, a colony first settled by Quaker immigrants, experienced its own period of slavery that lasted into the early 1800s. During the colonial period, Quakers themselves were frequent owners of slaves, although the Friends would ultimately emerge as the leading religious opponents of slavery. The Society of Friends had a long history of conflict with slavery. In 1676, founder George Fox had advised Quaker planters on the island of Barbados to free their slaves if they had proved good servants. Consider, he asked them, "if you were in the same [c]ondition as the [b]lacks are…who came as [s]trangers to you, and were sold to you as Slaves; now I say, if this should be the [c]ondition of you or yours, you [would] think it hard [m]easure; yea, and very great Bondage and Cruelty."[10]

Despite these appeals, during the early colonial years, many Quakers still owned slaves. Lucrative trade relations with fellow Friends in Barbados may have stifled some early antislavery sentiments. Abolitionist Quakers were a decided minority during their first fifty years in Pennsylvania. Nevertheless, early antislavery tracts published by outspoken Pennsylvania Quakers evoked stirring images of the sins of slavery. Slaveholders, opined Friend Benjamin Lay in 1737, "are the choicest Treasure the Devil can or has to bring out of his Lazaretto....By these Satan works Wonders [in] many ways." Those who "practise Tyranny and Oppression for Slave-keeping" assume "unjustly, Dominion over his Fellow-Creature's Liberty and Property, contrary to Law, Reason or Equity."[11]

William Southeby, who first publicly protested slavery in 1696, invoked the "Golden Rule," citing Matthew: those who "purchase...these negroes" appeared to him "to Contradict our Great Law-giver's holy precepts... where he saith, whatsoever ye would that men should do unto you, even so do ye unto them." He also felt that many slaveholders had grown lazy and greedy, noting, "We hardly know how to carry it on without Slaves." Southeby acknowledged that by freeing slaves, "we may not live altogether so high & full as now...by the oppression of these poor people," but he believed that Pennsylvanians would enjoy "more peace, and a clearer Conscience in the Sight of God." "I undoubtedly believe," he continued, "that the time is come, and comeing that one nation shall not oppress, nor one people another; nor make Slaves of Each other, neither that the Great and merciful God will have respect to any one Sort of People more than to another, either because they are Black or White or Taunie."[12]

Moral epiphanies grew in number as the century progressed. In 1743, Quaker John Woolman found himself reluctant to draw up a bill of sale for a slave woman when requested by his employer. "The thing was [s]udden," he wrote, "and though the thoughts of writing an Instrument of Slavery for one of my fellow creatures felt uneasie, yet I remembered I was hired by the year....So through weakeness I gave way, and wrote it, but at the [e]xecuting it I was so [a]fflicted in my mind, that I said...that I believed Slavekeeping to be a practice inconsistent with the Christian Religion."[13]

Like-minded Quakers became more involved in monthly, quarterly and yearly meetings. In what would become a model for future abolitionist organizing, antislavery Quakers climbed the ladders of influence within Friends meetinghouses, placing themselves in positions to enact antislavery measures. In 1752, abolitionist Anthony Benezet, a French Huguenot refugee turned Quaker, was appointed to the overseers of the press, a vital group of Friends who decided what tracts were consistent with Quaker belief and could therefore be published. Once entrenched, Benezet helped pass resolutions limiting and discouraging slaveholding among fellow Quakers and published antislavery tracts—a precursor to the American Anti-Slavery Society's "incendiary publications" of the 1830s. In the past, a previous generation of Quaker overseers had denied publication to antislavery tracts of reformers such as the vitriolic Benjamin Lay. In 1754, with Benezet and other abolitionists now overseers, they approved the publication of *Some Considerations on the Keeping of Negroes*, authored by John Woolman.[14]

As the French and Indian War engulfed western Pennsylvania in the 1750s, Benezet found more Quakers willing to speak out on slavery. John Churchman, a Philadelphia Quaker who embraced the faith's pacifist beliefs, was disturbed by the sudden arrival of war in what had been "a land of peace…not much concerned in war." Churchman watched as wagons carrying the bodies of the slain arrived in Philadelphia. In "a moment mine eyes were turned to the case of the poor enslaved Negroes," he wrote. No matter how "light a matter" some considered slavery, "it then appeared plain to me, that" those who held slaves "were partakers in iniquity, encouragers of war and the shedding of innocent blood, which is often the case, where those unhappy people are or have been captivated and brought away for slaves[.]" These were nothing less than sins, for which "the Lord has suffered this calamity and scourge to come upon them."[15]

Benezet, who himself took up the pen, aimed to persuade the next generation to steer clear of slavery. He hoped that antislavery tracts would "make as publick as possible for ye sake of ye youth, who have kept themselves hitherto clear of those People." Concurring with Benezet's crusade, in 1758, the Philadelphia yearly meeting ordered the formation of committees of "elder" Quakers to "visit and treat with all such Friends who have any Slaves." Among those making the rounds was John Woolman.[16]

Yet Quaker abolitionism did not develop in a vacuum. In the mid-eighteenth century, people of African descent—both enslaved and free—had a sizable presence throughout Philadelphia and much of British North America. Recent scholarship suggests that Benezet's writings may have been informed by interviews with African Americans. Their oral testimony to the cruelties of slave trade may very well account for the gripping detail found in his antislavery publications.[17]

Benezet continued his own authorial efforts into the 1760s. A tactful promoter, he appealed to the grand sense of British empire in his 1766 pamphlet titled *A Caution and Warning to Great Britain and Her Colonies, in a Short Representation of the Calamitous State of the Enslaved Negroes in the British Dominions*. His 1771 book decrying the slave trade, *Some Historical Account of Guinea*, was hailed by British abolitionists as "instrumental…in disseminating a proper knowledge and detestation of this trade." Navigating the chains of power, Benezet managed to get appropriations from the yearly meeting to cover the expense of printing some two thousand copies of his *A Caution and Warning* and sent "about Four Dozen" copies of the work back to the London meeting for distribution there. Benezet, notes one recent scholar, "wanted his pamphlet to reach people with the political power to take action against slavery, and to realize that goal he drew upon all the Quaker resources he could muster."[18] After a lengthy battle, in 1774, the Philadelphia yearly meeting banned slaveholding among Friends.[19]

Not all Quakers were as voracious as the likes of Woolman and Benezet. Many lived to regret their lack of activism. Graceanna Lewis's father died in 1824 with a deathbed confession that "he had allowed ill health to prevent him from becoming a member of the Abolition Society." As Graceanna and her siblings grew into maturity, she was surrounded by family, friends and neighbors who all opposed human bondage. "My Mother and her family were equally a[s] opposed to slavery," Lewis later recalled. "As we grew older, our associations were with Anti Slavery persons." Living in eastern Pennsylvania, noted abolitionists were not always elusive celebrities. "Those who were doing their best to Extinguish American Slavery, were our guests and our favored friends," she reminisced. Throughout her adolescence and adulthood, Lewis recalled with pride sheltering freedom seekers, most of whom had left the border slave states of Virginia, Maryland and Delaware.[20]

At the same time, African American activists—the sometimes partners of Quakers—launched moral appeals to end slavery, many of them emanating from the pulpit. Richard Allen, Absalom Jones, James Forten and Russell Parrott published pamphlets condemning both slavery and the racism that pervaded even many abolitionists. Above all, they emphasized their determination to seek futures in America. "We were *stolen* from our mother country and brought *here*," declared Allen, bishop of the African Methodist Episcopal (AME) Church in Philadelphia, the first black denomination in the United States. "Africans have made fortunes for thousands, who are yet unwilling to part with their services[.]"[21] By the turn of the nineteenth century, in Pennsylvania and elsewhere, Quakers and African Americans had lit the flame of reform that would soon inspire countless others.

CHAPTER 1

"THE IRON ENTERED MY SOUL"

BENJAMIN LUNDY AND THE MORAL CALLING

September 1809. Twenty-year-old Quaker Benjamin Lundy worked long days in a musky saddler's shop in Wheeling, Virginia, learning to cut leather to exact and precise patterns for a demanding clientele. An apprentice, Lundy took the sobriquet of *journeyman* quite literally—the New Jersey–born Quaker had left his father's farm in Sussex County, traveling through Pennsylvania and Ohio before finally settling down in Wheeling.

Saddles, harnesses and whips were in high demand among men headed westward with their families, livestock and very often slaves. Many of the customers who purchased Lundy's crafts were known as "slave drivers." The westward craze had paved the way for this class of men, whose business it was to march shackled slaves from the plantations of the upper South to new lands in the South and Southwest. Years of repetitive tobacco farming in the Chesapeake region had eroded the quality of the soil, and the once-dominant plantations of eastern Maryland and the Virginia tidewater now found more profit in selling slaves and their offspring than in farming.

"Coffles" of chained slaves became a common sight throughout the South. One seven-year-old boy recalled witnessing "the coffle of slaves… chained in couples on each side of a long chain which extended between them; the driver was some distance behind, with the wagon of supplies." The driver, who soon came into view, "furnished a long whip, such as is used in driving cattle, and goaded the reluctant and weary when their feet lagged on the long journey."[22] In his early thirties, William Seward—later a leading antislavery politician—encountered just such a group during a family vacation to Virginia. In the distance, a "cloud of dust was seen slowly coming down the road, from which proceeded a confused noise of moaning, weeping, and shouting." As this noise neared, it was revealed to be "[t]en naked little boys, between six and twelve years old, tied together, two and two, by their wrists…all fastened to a long rope, and followed by a tall, gaunt white man, who, with his long lash, whipped up the sad and weary little procession, drove it to the horse-trough to drink, and thence to a shed, where they lay down on the ground and sobbed and moaned themselves to sleep."[23]

Slave drivers were vital to the southern economy, although nonetheless shunned by self-righteous southern slaveholders as "the most utterly detestable of all Southern Yankees[.]" Slaveholders, who came to regard themselves as honorable patriarchs manifesting a "paternal" care over their slaves, frequently bemoaned the "miserly Negro Trader" who is "outwardly, a coarse ill-bred person, provincial in speech and manners, with a cross-looking phiz, a whiskey-tinctured nose, cold hard-looking eyes, a dirty tobacco-stained mouth, and shabby dress." Southern writer Daniel Hundley opined in 1860 that slave drivers "habitually" separate "parent from child, brother from sister, and husband from wife," yet they remain "the jolliest dogs alive," without showing the "least sign of remorse." Nevertheless, this did not preclude them from purchasing human chattel from these hated "Southern Yankees."[24]

Cruelty and slavery were nothing new in this frontier town. To a New Jersey–born Quaker, it was unconscionable. Benjamin Lundy stayed in Wheeling for four years while apprenticing with a saddler, a period that would profoundly shape both his life and, in turn, the destiny of his nation. Although Lundy created for himself a narrowly focused world, centered on the precise "mechanics" of his trade, his work in the servant class, he later reflected, improved his character and mental "faculties" and refined "the principles that have since guided me in my public labours."

Being a Quaker, however, never left Lundy. Although he was lodging with a man whom he described as a "regular gambler" and "associated" himself with "wild, fashionable youths," Lundy retained the plain dress so characteristic of Quaker beliefs about modesty and simplicity, attended Quaker meetings, "shunned every species of gambling and frolicking" and remained a voracious reader of books. Like many devout Quakers before him, Lundy's self-emergence and religious convictions clashed with the institution of slavery, which he saw all around him. In Wheeling, he would later write, "I first became acquainted with the wrongs of the slave." He found the trading town to be "a great thoroughfare for the traffickers in human flesh. Their 'coffles' passed through the place frequently. My heart

An abolitionist rendering of the slave trade, depicting coffled slaves in the shadow of the nation's capital. *Library of Congress.*

was deeply grieved at the gross abomination; I heard the wail of the captive; I felt his pang of distress; and the iron entered my soul."[25]

Night after night, day after day, the image recurred in his mind. It stayed with him forever—the "droves of a dozen or twenty ragged men, chain together and driven through the streets, *bare-headed* and *bare-footed, in mud and snow*, by remorseless 'SOUL SELLERS,' with horsewhips and bludgeons in their hands!!" Confronting the beliefs of his Quaker upbringing head-on, Lundy vowed to "break at least one link of that ponderous chain of oppression."[26]

Lundy left Wheeling after four years and moved to Mount Pleasant, Ohio. There, he married and had "two beautiful little daughters." Prosperity, he wrote, "seemed to smile before me." Nonetheless, he recalled, "I enjoyed no peace of mind," and as he lamented "the sad condition of the slave…I at length concluded that I *must* act." In 1815, he and "five or six" others formed an antislavery group christened the Union Humane Society, started in Lundy's own home. Within a few months, membership had swelled to five hundred. Putting pen to paper, Lundy drafted an antislavery circular that he published under a pseudonym. Drawing on many long-held Quaker grievances about slavery, Lundy stressed that ending the slave trade was not enough, "as the seeds of the evil system had been sown in our soil, and were springing up and producing increase." A talent for writing quickly discerned, Lundy accepted an invitation to edit a paper in St. Louis, Missouri, then a hotbed of national debate over slavery.[27]

IN THE LATE FALL of 1819, Lundy stepped off into the streets of St. Louis, a swirling frontier town already at the center of a tense national debate. Congress had first begun to consider the question of Missouri's statehood in 1818. However, in February 1819, New York congressman James Tallmadge Jr. introduced an amendment restricting the "further introduction" of slavery into the soon-to-be state and freeing children of all existing slaves at age twenty-five. The amendment quickly sparked a violent debate in the halls of Congress. Many northern congressmen rallied in support of Tallmadge. They stressed Missouri's opportunity "to set in motion the machine of free government beyond the Mississippi." Drawing on the Northwest Ordinance of 1787—which barred slavery from any and all territories northwest of the Ohio River—and the understanding that Congress's power to admit new states was discretionary, they argued that the federal government possessed the authority to restrict slavery in the new states. Rather than out of sympathy for the slave, they claimed that slavery scorned and discouraged free labor performed by whites.

Virginia's Philip Barbour responded that the expansion of slavery westward—resulting in its "diffusion" throughout a greater territory—would inevitably result in better conditions for slaves. An inflamed Barbour went on to accuse Tallmadge of attempting to keep southerners out of Missouri. If slavery was barred from the incoming state, southerners—who, Barbour alleged, had a "personal" attachment to their slaves as their "most valued" and "most favored property"—could not enter a free Missouri, effectively closing off the new state to southern migration.

Benjamin Lundy, America's leading abolitionist prior to 1830. *Massachusetts Historical Society.*

Making that decision for Missouri, Barbour continued, would only make Missouri "less sovereign." The original thirteen colonies had all decided the question of slavery independent of the federal government, he argued, so why should Missouri be any different? Missouri's non-voting delegate to Congress, John Scott, concurred. The people of Missouri, he declared, "knew their own rights" and would not have them wrested away. "[I]f admitted into the national family," Scott announced, it would be as "equals" or not at all.[28] Now thirty years old, Lundy thus found himself "on the great scene of discussion, and in the midst of those whose interests were most involved. My feelings prompted me to engage in the controversy." Through late nights spent hunched over his desk, scrawling on pieces of rough parchment paper, Lundy drafted "an exposition…of the evils of slavery."[29] Not concealing his admiration, Lundy would name his eldest son, Charles Tallmadge Lundy, after the New Yorker.[30]

Many miles to the east in Washington, passions spilled over in the heated confrontations on the House floor. Threats of disunion mounted as the delicate republic seemed on the verge of division. Georgia's Thomas Cobb bluntly accused Tallmadge of having "kindled a fire which all the waters of the ocean cannot put out, which seas of blood can only extinguish." Undeterred, Tallmadge retorted: "If blood is necessary to extinguish any fire which I have assisted to kindle, I can assure the gentlemen, while I regret the necessity, I shall not forbear to contribute my mite."[31] In response, Virginia's eccentric, opium-consuming Congressman John Randolph declared bombastically: "God has given us the Missouri and the devil shall not take it from us."[32]

Through the efforts of then–House speaker Henry Clay, a compromise was reached, admitting Maine as a free state to counterbalance Missouri's admission as a slave state. Although Clay's reputation grew as a result, the compromise was a defeat for moral abolitionists such as Lundy. The compromise also drew an east–west line from Missouri's southern border to the western reaches of the United States (then in dispute), prohibiting slavery north of the line but permitting it south of it. It was this fact that Thomas Jefferson eyed with great concern as the smoke dissipated from the Missouri affair. "[I]t is hushed indeed for the moment," he wrote from Monticello, "but this is a reprieve only,—not a final sentence." A "geographical line, coinciding with a marked principle, moral and political, once conceived and held up to the angry passions of men, will never be obliterated."[33]

ALTHOUGH LUNDY LEFT ST. Louis having failed to convince Missourians to rid themselves of slavery, he was by no means a defeated man. Newly energized that slavery had become a national issue, he next wandered through Tennessee, attempting to set up shop for his antislavery serial, the *Genius of Universal Emancipation*. In 1823, he even wrote a letter to Tennessee's most famous citizen (and slaveholder), General Andrew Jackson, then widely presumed to be a candidate for the presidency.

"I am the editor of a periodical work entitled the 'Genius of Universal Emancipation,'" he wrote, "published in this place, and devoted exclusively to the subject of negro slavery as it exists in this Republic." Although a "purely political" subject, Lundy assured Jackson, "I am no factionist; I proceed upon independent principles; and if I know myself, have nothing but the good of my country in view." He sought to see "justice done on every hand, believing that this, alone, will preserve us, as a nation, amid the agonizing pangs and convulsive throes of corrupted, diseased, and expiring Empires."

"It is understood that thee will be a candidate for the Presidential chair of the Untied States, at the next election.—And as I consider it a matter of great importance that our chief magistrate be a man who is disposed to use his influence in bringing about a gradual abolition of slavery in every part of the Republic, I would be glad…to have thy sentiments on the subject." Politics in the early American republic were intended to be a cat-and-mouse game of "disinterested" politicians who were drafted and put forth by their "friends" (usually carefully arranged committees of political allies). Candor about ambitions was a major breech of political protocol.

Choosing his words carefully, Lundy began to write his next sentence: "I am not about to make any promises of…support, &c. even if thee should satisfy me on this point; but I will just observe that impartial persons in some parts of the country have requested me to inform them whether thee is, or is not, a friend to universal liberty." He paused, read the sentence over and decided he had not been specific enough. In parentheses, he scrawled "free states" to specify what "parts of the country" would appreciate antislavery views. He read the sentence over again and this time underlined "<u>universal liberty</u>," a phrase that he felt was synonymous with the general's own legendary career of serving his country.[34] Unsurprisingly, Jackson paid little heed to Lundy's hints at support—assertions that Jackson knew were hardly backed in any political reality. Unbeknownst at the time to either Lundy or Jackson, it would be another full decade before abolitionists and antislavery organizers would begin to exert real influence over local, state and finally national elections.

Nonetheless, Lundy remained, settling at Greeneville in eastern Tennessee. Unlike many abolitionists who followed him, Lundy preferred to live in slaveholding regions, hoping to convince local residents wherever he went of the inherent sinfulness of slavery. In the words of his biographer, Lundy sought to reach the very slaveholders "who had it within their power to abolish slavery."[35] Drawing strength from the presence of antislavery Quakers in eastern Tennessee and western North Carolina, he understood

President Andrew Jackson (1829–37) was a southerner, slave owner and Indian fighter. He was generally unpopular among abolitionists, especially in South Central Pennsylvania. *Library of Congress.*

the importance of publicizing dissent within the slave states. "[T]he bare existence of a Manumission society, is an important thing," Lundy wrote in the *Genius* in 1822. "[I]t raises a kind of ensign with something like this inscription, 'slavery is wrong, it is an unreasonable violation of justice, and opposed to our best interest.'"[36] Twenty-one states and territories soon received the *Genius*, creating a vast network of subscribers, agents and promoters, prompting discussions on slavery and antislavery efforts throughout the country.

What distinguished Lundy from other abolitionists was his determination to appeal to southerners' own economic self-interest. While slavery might be a great source of wealth "for individual planters and slave traders," his biographer synthesized, Lundy would argue that "society at large" is "stifled" economically. In the *Genius*, Lundy tackled topics ranging from soil depletion to the "comparative value of slave and free labor," complete with lengthy statistical analyses. Although compellingly written, his pitches did little to sway southerners moving into newly christened western states. In the words of Lundy's biographer, in such "a highly individualistic age arguments about the social good, however well documented, were not very compelling." Others who might have found Lundy's economic appeal convincing nonetheless remained attached to slavery, believing it "a necessary means of maintaining white supremacy."[37]

Seeking to broaden his audience, in the fall of 1823, Lundy attended an antislavery convention in Philadelphia. There, the western journeyman-editor mingled with wealthy philanthropists, whose conservative approach to abolition dismayed Lundy. They were more philanthropists than activists, in Lundy's view. He soon recognized, however, the advantages of setting up shop along the interconnected and populous Eastern Seaboard and left the meeting determined to relocate there. He chose Baltimore, where he arrived in 1824.[38]

In the midst of a contentious 1824 presidential election, Lundy was settling into Baltimore, enraptured with the idea of setting up an antislavery serial in a major East Coast city. Much like during his time in Tennessee, Lundy also set about convincing local Marylanders of the "genius" of emancipation. In August 1825, he and a group of close friends established the Maryland Anti-Slavery Society, seeking a peaceful end to slavery through political means. "THE BALLOT BOX MUST BE RESORTED TO," Lundy loudly proclaimed in the *Genius*. "This will be the ONLY means…by which slavery can be annihilated without commotion, rapine, and indescribable woe." His pleas were met with increasing hostility. On the streets of Baltimore, a city with a large enslaved population, Lundy was frequently the target of violence by slaveholders and proslavery men.[39]

BY THE LATE 1820s, Lundy had given up trying to convince southerners to abolish slavery for their own good. He now sought to appeal to northerners and in 1828 embarked upon a tour of the northeastern states. Lundy's northern circuit came at a new time in American life. Among evangelicals, the Second Great Awakening cast religion as a centerpiece of their identity. Around the same time, a new print culture placed emphasis on the spoken or written word, encouraging theological and moral discussions that involved both men and women. Reform was the word of the day, and both major political parties claimed to be agents of moral, social and political reform. In 1828, Andrew Jackson ascended to the presidency on the platform of "Jackson and Reform."[40]

Lundy's goal was to mobilize local "Abolition and Manumission Societies…to have memorials signed by as many of the citizens of their vicinity as practicable, and forwarded to Congress, praying the Abolition of Slavery in the District of Columbia." Through public lectures at Friends meetinghouses, churches and public lecture halls, he hoped to enlighten listeners to the economic benefits of free labor over slave labor. Also eager to capitalize on America's new print culture, Lundy had set aside funds for "publishing Books, Pamphlets and Tracts, that may have a tendency to enlighten and correct public opinion on the subject of Slavery."[41]

His younger half sister, Lydia Shotwell Lundy, then living in New Jersey, rejoiced to see "My Dear Brother Benjamin[.]" She attended his meetings at Mount Holly and Burlington, New Jersey, where she witnessed firsthand his grassroots efforts to abolish slavery. "The meeting was organized," she wrote, "and appointed a committee to join the Committee of Mount Holly in drawing up a form of a Memorial to Congress, Praying for the Abolition of Slavery in the district of Columbia.…It is now circulating for signatures."[42]

THE ABUNDANCE OF WESTERN land did more than open the door for slavery's expansion. It also revolutionized the American family. For generations, families had lived continuously on the same farms. The opening of the West and the establishment of the General Land Office—even with its faults—offered a host of new opportunities to young people, who before would have been confined to the East Coast, if not to the farm they had been born on. Family connections now spread out, spanning hundreds of miles to the west and southwest; letter writing, along with word of mouth carried by passersby, became the main way of communicating significant events such as pregnancies, births, sicknesses and deaths. The letters of early nineteenth-century Americans are filled with such essential details, almost always concluding with a request for similar "gossip" from their recipient.

The Lundy family was no different. In the early 1830s, Lydia Lundy moved to York Springs, Pennsylvania, a Quaker stronghold in northern Adams County, where she found work as an instructor at a boarding school for girls. There she married Joel Wierman, a Quaker with deep roots in the area known locally as "Quaker Valley." The dutiful and doting brother, Benjamin kept up a steady trail of correspondence with his beloved half sister, his letters postmarked from whichever city he happened to be in at the time. In May 1831, shortly after her marriage to Wierman, Benjamin wrote to her:

> *After leaving Washington again, (probably in 4 or 5 months from this date) I shall shape my course pretty directly to you[r] part of the country. I shall not go far away until I see what kind of a home my dear sister has.…If I am not exceedingly deceived, thee has a kind and worthy husband. I have esteemed him very highly ever since I became acquainted with him, but circumstances forbade my expressing the kindly feeling of my heart towards him. I knew however that he has good sense enough to approve, rather than condemn, my seeming taciturnity. The case is now altered,—and I tender him the assurance of brother's kindest affection. And thee must impress it on his mind.*
>
> *When I sat down I did not think of writing half so much: but as I forgot to stop sooner, thee must pardon my prolixity.*
> *Sincerely, Dear Sister,*
> *I am Thy Loving Brother,*
> *B. Lundy*[43]

Joel and Lydia Lundy Wierman, as they appeared around the time of the Civil War. The half sister of Benjamin Lundy, Lydia had an abolitionist pedigree that was never in doubt. *Private collection, Marcy Morris.*

Lundy's hearty approval of his new brother-in-law no doubt stemmed in part from Wierman's own antislavery activities. Joel, in his mid-forties, had been helping runaway slaves dating back to 1819, if not earlier. Within a few years, Wierman would go public as a signer of the constitution of the Adams County Anti-Slavery Society, which held alternating meetings in both Gettysburg and York Springs.[44] In one of his few letters that survive, Wierman reveals himself to be a devout Quaker as well as a persistent abolitionist, signing his letter, "I am thine in the cause of the oppressed."[45] His sister Phebe lived nearby with her husband, Joel's brother-in-law, William Wright. Together, William and Phebe were among the most prolific conductors on the Underground Railroad throughout the entire country. Although not the primary "conductor" in the York Springs vicinity, Wierman continued to share the burden with his brother-in-law, frequently concealing freedom seekers in his home.[46]

Lydia remained active too. She, like many other women, found in the abolitionist movement a political space to push for moral reform. In December 1833, Quaker Lucretia Mott had spoken to great fanfare before a largely male antislavery convention in Philadelphia, her "sweet female voice" emanating throughout the hall. "She had risen and commenced speaking, but was hesitating," recalled one attendee, "because she feared the larger part of the Convention not being Quakers might think it 'a shame for a woman to speak in a church,' and that she was unwilling to give them offence. Her beautiful countenance was radiant with the thoughts that had moved her to speak." The delegates welcomed Mott warmly and applauded her "impressive and effective speech" as one of the highlights of the convention.[47]

A great proponent of women's involvement in politics and reform movements, Lundy wrote, "I believe that Providence design'd my sect for a greater sphere of usefulness than a…consern of domestic life alone…and if you woman [*sic*] would look around them with the tenderness and compassion peculiar to our sect, they would see much for them

Lucretia Mott, a Quaker reformer, was a powerful antislavery lecturer who supported female involvement in social discourse. *Library of Congress*.

ABOLITIONISTS OF SOUTH CENTRAL PENNSYLVANIA

to be engaged of Much usefulness to the Great Human family." She believed that women should "apply in our own hearts with this Query, What can I do, to assist the Many strugling [*sic*] victims of Misery and suffering?"[48]

Little concerning Lydia Lundy Wierman's antislavery activities survives; however, her family connection to one of the country's leading abolitionists garnered her no shortage of attention. The fact that she was singled out as a reliable contact by a distant antislavery office speaks volumes. In August 1837, the Philadelphia branch of the Pennsylvania Anti-Slavery Society forwarded her a petition designed to collect women's signatures and then be forwarded to Congress. The printed heading read:

> *To the Senate and House of Representatives in Congress assembled: The undersigned, women of* Adams County Pa. *deeply convinced of the sinfulness of Slavery, and keenly aggrieved by its existence in a part of our country over which Congress possesses exclusive jurisdiction, in all cases whatsoever, do most earnestly petition your body, immediately to abolish Slavery in the District of Columbia, and the Territories of the United States, and the Slave Trade between the States.*

Huldah Justice, the Philadelphia operative who sent the petitions, informed another recipient that "our object is to get at least one petition into every township" in Adams County, believing that "there must be a sufficient number of females in the township[s] favorably disposed towards the coercion which we are engaged, to render the requisite aid, if I knew where they are to be found." All females over sixteen years of age were permitted to sign.[49]

By the 1830s, however, Lydia's "Dear Brother Benjamin" was no longer the country's leading abolitionist editor. That role—and the consequences that went with it—belonged to Lundy's former apprentice, William Lloyd Garrison.

CHAPTER 2

"THE SCALES FELL FROM MY EYES"

WILLIAM LLOYD GARRISON AND CUMBERLAND COUNTY ABOLITIONISTS

Danger surrounded John Peck on all sides. A black man in a state that was ever-so-slowly freeing its slaves, he was part of a tenuous minority. Slave catchers routinely made trips into the border regions of southern Pennsylvania, often capturing and enslaving blacks who had been born free. Slaves from nearby Maryland, Virginia and Washington, D.C., fled to southern Pennsylvania as the nearest place of refuge. It was, by all means, a dangerous and uncertain boundary in the divide between freedom and slavery.

By the early 1820s, Pennsylvania was home to fewer than five hundred slaves. The state had passed a Gradual Abolition of Slavery in 1780, stating that all slaves born after March 1780 would be free on their twenty-eighth birthday. Tragically, the law left the several thousand men and women born prior to the act's passage in bondage for life. The town of Carlisle, in the south central part of the state, had been home to roughly eighty slaves since the days of the Revolution. There, African American slaves had been employed as blacksmiths, coachmen and agricultural laborers.

Carlisle's slave-owning class looked apprehensively at a large black population that was gaining more freedom every year. Their concern only mounted among the close confines of the rural Pennsylvania town, where slaves and free blacks mingled and conversed. In 1794, slaveholder William Miller advertised "a stout young Mulatto man, about 21 or 22 years old," who was to be sold "for want of having sufficient employment." By law, the man would be free in about six years. Miller, however, wanted to sell him to

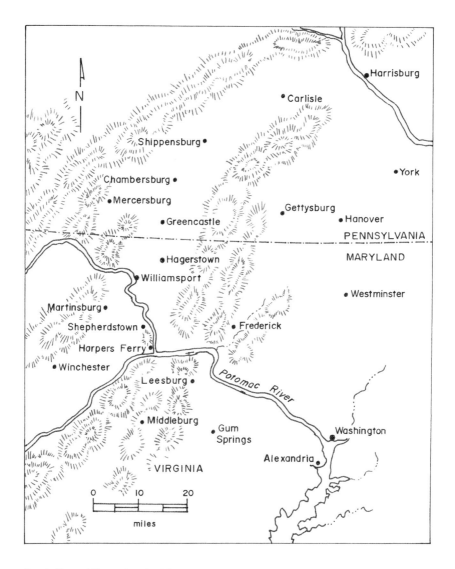

South Central Pennsylvania. *Map by John Heiser.*

a farmer who could "look after him" and "keep him from bad company." His man "can plow, chop and drive a waggon [*sic*], and may be made a very valuable servant."[50] Rather than prepare so-called term slaves for freedom, slaveholders were content to grasp every legal method available to keep blacks in bondage for as long as possible. Theophile Cazenove, a Dutch traveler, met farmers on the road leading south from Carlisle to Gettysburg who complained loudly "about the mis-conduct, thefts, etc., of the now free negroes."[51]

Come 1821, when John Peck arrived in Carlisle, the throes of slavery were slowly vanishing. Each year, a succession of "term-slaves" turned twenty-eight years old and became free. Freedom, however, was a concept with a limited meaning. Slavery still lingered on, and the local papers still advertised slaves for sale. One April 1823 notice read:

> FOR SALE
> A healthy Negro Girl,
> Thirteen years old, to serve until 28—very smart and large of her age. She is offered for sale for the want of employment.[52]

For Peck and other free African Americans, the color of their skin limited their economic mobility. Black males generally found work as barbers, coach drivers and other service-related occupations.

Peck resided in a "small log house" on Church Alley, in the heart of Carlisle. He was a barber but also kept a cow—valued at ten dollars—on his lot for milk. By 1829, Peck had been fairly successful at plying his trade and was able to purchase a "1st rate" horse, which was valued at seventy dollars.[53]

A FIERCE OPPONENT OF slavery, Peck was in an ideal position to work both publicly and covertly to precipitate slavery's undoing. As the 1830s dawned, he and other active African Americans capitalized on growing support from rural northern whites. The new decade ushered in a vast revolution throughout the North. Antislavery northerners, formerly few and far between, had taken pains to organize themselves. At Boston in 1832, William Lloyd Garrison and a handful of devoted followers had formed the New England Anti-Slavery Society. In December 1833, Garrison and others made the trip to Philadelphia, where, with delegates from a slew of northern states, they established the American Anti-Slavery Society.

A grassroots movement, the abolitionists drew their greatest strength from the rural hinterlands of northern states. Places like upstate New York (near Syracuse, Utica and Auburn), western Massachusetts and the Quaker strongholds of southern and eastern Pennsylvania provided tens of thousands of recruits to the cause. Support came in various forms. One way of staying apprised of new developments was investing in subscriptions to the growing number of antislavery newspapers, magazines and journals. At the county level, rural activists formed local chapters of the American Anti-Slavery Society. Conventions and public gatherings became more frequent, and throughout the 1830s, slavery, for the first time, was at the front and center of American politics.

Among rural white activists, the driving force behind the movement was faith. There, the antislavery crusade was very much a religious movement. Evangelical Christianity was sweeping rural America, instilling in thousands the belief that they were active agents in shaping both their own destiny as well as that of their nation. Ideas about predestination were fading in favor of belief in individual agency. Forty-four-year-old William Goodell, the editor of *The Friend of Man*, an abolitionist serial published in Utica, New York, asked his readers: "With the Bible in our hands,—with consciences in our breasts,—especially, with the Spirit of truth in our hearts…how is it possible that we could ever have been anything but zealous abolitionists, without the most flagrant sin against God?"[54]

In the eyes of many abolitionists, the antislavery movement was nothing less than a crusade, with no lack of biblical overtones. "But a few years ago," reflected the *Spirit of Liberty*, an abolitionist paper out of Pittsburgh, "and the nation's mind was resting easily on the entire subject of slavery—now thousands are enlisted under the Anti-Slavery banners—*Soldiers for the War*. We have come out, and, in the face of the world, taken our stand on the *Lord's side*."[55]

Ridiculed as extremists and fanatics, unrealistic super-reformers who would disrupt social norms, abolitionists chose to embrace the criticisms. "The abolitionist, if he is sincere, must be extravagant," responded one Massachusetts author. Speaking to the evangelical impulse, he wrote that if one "believed his immortal welfare depended *on reforming other people's sins*, he could hardly be blamed for any extravagance of action."[56] To defend "the right of free discussion," a Rhode Island antislavery convention determined, "is to be an Abolitionist in principle and in practice." Confident that "[t]he contest now raging in this country must inevitably drive every advocate of free discussion into the adoption of Anti-Slavery principles and the support of Anti-Slavery measures," they declared that there "can be no abiding middle ground between universal despotism and universal freedom."[57]

"Sir, I am an abolitionist," penned Asa Mahan, president of Oberlin College in northern Ohio, the first school in the country to admit students of both races. "In every station and relation in life, I would be known as such, while a single slave groans beneath the oppressor's yoke, or bleeds beneath the oppressor's scourge."[58] "I am an abolitionist" became a statement of defiance, holding up a higher law that abolitionists believed justified their efforts. "I am an abolitionist," declared Reverend James T. Woodbury at a New Hampshire convention in 1834. "I feel that more than 2,000,000 of my fellow beings, and most of them my countrymen, native born Americans, are robbed of their rights....And I cannot close my eyes, and shut my mouth, and hold my peace, or cry, 'All is well,' 'All is right.' 'The laws and the constitution say so.' No, no. Human legislation can never amend the law of God."[59] "The cause of emancipation is identified with prayer," declared Reverend Theodore S. Wright, a black pastor at a New York City Presbyterian church. "Did you ever see an abolitionist without prayer?"[60]

Interracial coordination also became more pronounced than ever before. Papers run by white activists, such as Goodell's *The Friend of Man*, began reprinting columns from an array of black papers being established throughout the North, such as the *Colored American* (also known as the *Weekly Advocate*) in New York City. Establishing a rapport that was surprisingly effective at dismantling racial and social prejudices, whites and blacks would generally work well together, both in public activism and in clandestine activity along the famed Underground Railroad.

Charles Bennett Ray and Samuel E. Cornish, the founders of the *Colored American*, understood the importance of incorporating black voices into the antislavery movement. Not only did slavery most directly affect people of color, but they, too, sought to be active agents in the determination of their own fate. Neither whites nor blacks could bring about emancipation alone— it would require a concerted effort. Ray and Cornish stressed just that. "Because no class of men, however pious and benevolent can take our place in the great work of redeeming our character and removing our disabilities [slavery, prejudice]. They may identify themselves with us, and enter into our sympathies. Still it is ours to will and to do." They hoped that the *Colored American* might become "an appropriate engine" of "facts and instruction." "[I]t will tell tales of woe, both in the church and out of the church; such as are calculated to make the heart to bleed and the ear to burn. It will bring to light many hidden things, which must be revealed and repented of, or this nation must perish."[61]

Tensions inevitably arose. Many blacks felt white abolitionists were at times lofty, condescending and self-righteous. But prominent black leaders such as Ray and Cornish sought to soothe hard feelings. "The colored man who does not hold the person, the character and the doings, of American Abolitionists in the highest estimation, is unworthy [of] the form he wears, and the standing he holds among the reputable of his race," the *Colored American* thundered in September 1837. "Upon the Altar of conscience and of God, they have placed their lives, their property, and their sacred honor— willing to sink or swim, live or die, by their principles."[62]

As A BARBER, PECK was among the most influential group of working-class blacks in the North. Barbering put blacks in touch with clientele of both races, allowing for eavesdropping, all the while earning a steady stream of income, with which they could support black civic interests. In the view of one scholar, barbers "formed a vanguard in the struggle for black civil rights."[63]

For like-minded customers, Peck was well stocked with the latest antislavery literature. It was in Peck's barbershop that James Miller McKim, a Carlisle native and Dickinson College student, first picked up a copy of the *Liberator*, William Lloyd Garrison's antislavery serial.

GARRISON WAS A REFORMER with a chip on his shoulder. He was born in 1807 along the Massachusetts coast, and when he was three his father deserted his mother and four siblings. As a young boy, William Lloyd fought an uphill battle to keep his family solvent and together, working odd jobs and hustling his mother's homemade products. However, harsh reality set in, and the Garrison children were split up to live among different households. In 1818, at thirteen years old, Garrison became an apprentice at the printing office of the *Newburyport Herald*, where he acquired the "arts and mysteries" of setting type and composing editorials.

After leaving the *Herald*, Garrison happened to be staying in Boston when Benjamin Lundy arrived there in March 1828. Each impressed the other with his candor, principles and argument, even where they differed. Lundy, anxious to continue his lecture circuit, offered Garrison the editorship of his *Genius of Universal Emancipation*—provided he would move to Baltimore. Garrison quickly agreed.

Garrison appreciated Lundy's "ardent and unselfish devotion to his work" and his "simple-minded Quaker" lifestyle. His editorials breathed an intense passion, coupled with harsh language previously unseen. Garrison's new confrontational style turned away some of the southern readership Lundy had spent years cultivating.

William Lloyd Garrison rose to prominence with his fiery editorials and unrelenting attacks on slavery. He soon passed Lundy as the nation's most famous abolitionist. *Library of Congress.*

Unsurprisingly, the Massachusetts editor made no shortage of enemies. After insulting the captain of a slave ship then docked in Baltimore's harbor, Garrison was convicted for libel and sentenced to six months in jail. Undeterred, he continued to edit the *Genius* from his prison cell. "It is my shame that I have done so little of the people of color," he wrote, declaring his own martyrdom. "A few white victims must be sacrificed to open the eyes of this nation, and to show the tyranny of our laws. I am willing to be persecuted, imprisoned, and bound for advocating African rights, and I should deserve to be a slave myself, if I shrunk from that duty or danger."[64]

When Lundy changed the *Genius* from a weekly to a monthly periodical, Garrison left for Boston. There, he worked with black leaders, raising money to finance a new paper dedicated to immediate abolition. It would be bold and assertive, holding nothing back, contrary to Lundy's moderate tactics. He published his first issue on New Year's Day 1831, signaling to the world a new chapter in the antislavery movement.[65]

Urgency was the theme of Garrison's writing. Americans, he believed, were sleeping on the precipice of moral abomination—the alarm had to be sounded.

I am aware that many object to the severity of my language, but is there not cause for severity? I will be as harsh as truth, and as uncompromising as justice. On this subject, I do not wish to think, or speak, or write, with moderation. No! no! Tell a man whose house is on fire to give a moderate alarm; tell him to moderately rescue his wife from the hands of the ravisher; tell the mother to gradually extricate her babe from the fire into which it has fallen;—but urge me not to use moderation in a cause like the present. I am in earnest—I will not equivocate—I will not excuse—I will not retreat a single inch—AND I WILL BE HEARD.[66]

In Peck's Carlisle barbershop, McKim found Garrison's *Liberator* "filled with discussion of the subject of slavery," a subject "to which my attention had never before been directed....Its vigor of style and the boldness of its argument were striking....I took it home with me, read it carefully, and came back the next day to talk about it."

In their ensuing conversation, McKim engaged Peck about colonization, a popular solution endorsed by leading statesmen such as former president James Monroe and Secretary of State Henry Clay. Colonization proposed to gradually free and then resettle enslaved African Americans elsewhere. The American Colonization Society, which boasted Clay as its president, had founded a colony called Liberia on the western coast of Africa for this very purpose. The premise of colonization—that, once freed, the two races could not live together in peace—was hotly disputed by leading African American intellectuals in the North, as well as by many of their abolitionist allies. As the pair discussed these issues, "[a]n argument arose," McKim recalled, at which point Peck procured a pamphlet recently published by Garrison entitled *Thoughts on Colonization*.

"I read it at one sitting," McKim later remembered.

> *The scales fell from my eyes. The whole truth was revealed to me. The evil of slavery, the vulgar cruelty of prejudice against color, the duty of the country and of every man in it toward the black man, were as plain as if they had been written out before me in letters of fire. From that time to this, I have been an Abolitionist. From that time to this, I have regarded my friend JOHN PECK, the colored barber, as one of my best benefactors.*[67]

In an era before the Internet and modern mass communications, print was king. The antislavery movement's success depended on individuals such as Peck disseminating abolitionist material to young, open-minded northerners. Peck was well read, subscribing to a variety of periodicals and journals, and a voracious reader of the works of leading luminaries in the movement. In January 1837, the *Weekly Advocate* (the forerunner to Ray and Cornish's *Colored American*) listed John Peck of Carlisle as an "agent" for the paper.[68] As McKim's account indicates, Peck had been actively promoting abolitionist serials for several years by that time.

Miller McKim, as he soon become to be known, rose rapidly through the ranks of the antislavery elite. In the fall of 1836, he was recruited as an agent for the rapidly expanding American Anti-Slavery Society, tasked with traveling the country on a speaking and publicity blitz. In addition to the lecturing circuit, McKim was also charged with distributing literature, organizing local chapters and collecting donations. It was work John Peck had been doing in Carlisle for several years.

Working as an antislavery lecturer was no glorious life. McKim received eight dollars a week, along with travel expenses, and regularly endured rudimentary arrangements and lukewarm receptions. Traveling through Pennsylvania, New Jersey and Delaware, he braved hostile hecklers and mobs, while dodging volleys of tomatoes, eggs, trash and stones that were hurled his way. In Gettysburg, he was nearly prevented from speaking until the town's state representative, Thaddeus Stevens, stepped in with the promise that he would personally prosecute any would-be assailants "to the very door of the penitentiary."

James Miller McKim, a Carlisle native, rose to national prominence as an abolitionist operating out of Philadelphia. *Boston Public Library.*

As part of his travels, McKim visited Washington, the site of so much abolitionist angst. Based on his visit there, he authored two letters to the *Emancipator* in New York, which were later published as a fourteen-page pamphlet titled *A Sketch of the Slave Trade in the District of Columbia*. In it, he spoke of the horrors of visiting a "*Slave-factory*," describing in intimate detail a "pen" no larger than "about 40 feet square, enclosed partly by the walls of the out buildings, and partly by high jail walls built for the purpose." In a separate "cellar…of about 25 feet square, were about 30 slaves of all ages, sizes, and colors. I noticed one young girl of about 12 years of age," penned McKim, "who seemed quite white, and another a little child about two years old, of the same shade, and one of the most beautiful children I ever saw." The sight was too much for McKim. "The guilt! the shame! the heartlessness!" he wrote, "the *hypocrisy* of this nation!"[69]

Within a few years, McKim opted for the less arduous role of publishing agent for the Pennsylvania Anti-Slavery Society. Working out of Philadelphia, he helped raise the $40,000 that was used to build Pennsylvania Hall, intended to be both a publishing center as well as a symbolic central meeting place for the society.[70] However, on May 17, 1838, within days of its opening, the building was torched by an anti-abolition mob. For its brief existence, Pennsylvania Hall had been the editorial headquarters of the *Pennsylvania Freeman*, the society's financially troubled

Pennsylvania Hall, a prominent symbol of abolitionism in Philadelphia, was torched by a mob within days of its opening in May 1838. *Library of Congress.*

paper. Its editor, John Greenleaf Whittier, barely escaped the building with his life.[71] Ostensibly filling the role of law-abiding public advocate, McKim in fact worked around the law when he felt the means justified the end. In Chester County, Graceanna Lewis recalled that McKim was "ready to assist us, when occasion required, either with advice, or with the means of purchasing Tickets on the Reading Rail Road, when it was Safe to use," to transport freedom seekers to Philadelphia.[72]

IN THE MEANTIME, PECK formed the Carlisle Anti-Slavery Society. Of modest size, the group failed to generate any significant buzz in Carlisle papers or surviving documents; however, the society did send delegates—Peck included—to an 1837 convention in Harrisburg to organize the Pennsylvania Anti-Slavery Society.[73]

Part of a national push to organize state and local antislavery societies, the convention was held in Harrisburg from January 31 to February 3, 1837. Alongside hundreds of abolitionists from throughout Pennsylvania, a number of out-of-state attendees rounded out the convention. Among them was John Greenleaf Whittier, a poet from the Massachusetts countryside.[74] In Boston, Whittier had already established himself as the poet laureate of the antislavery movement. Whittier could have led a profitable and prominent life on his poetic works alone. As if that were not enough, his name was also tossed around as a contender for Congress. But his heartfelt devotion to the abolition of slavery could not be silenced or demurred. Several years earlier, Whittier had been among the delegates who had traveled to Philadelphia in December 1833 to participate in the first national antislavery convention.[75] Also in attendance was an ailing Benjamin Lundy, who, in poor health for age forty-eight, seemed almost an apparition of the past.[76] Nevertheless, Lundy enjoyed the company of his brother-in-law, Joel Wierman, and Wierman's neighbor William Wright, who were accredited delegates representing the Adams County Anti-Slavery Society.[77]

Once gaveled in, the Harrisburg convention took particular aim at Washington, D.C.[78] With 40,000 residents, it paled in comparison to the great cities of America's East Coast such as New York and Philadelphia (each home to more than 300,000) and Boston (home to over 100,000). Population was not its only setback. Words could hardly convey the condition of the capital city. One journalist was shocked to find the capitol located seemingly "in the midst of wilderness." English author Charles Dickens dubbed it "the City of Magnificent Intentions," a tribute to its unfinished appearance. The Englishman was amused by its "streets…that only want houses" and "public buildings that need but a public to be complete." One resident unabashedly summed up the condition of the city, describing it as "a place of wide, unbuilt areas of land, oftentimes dreary commons, wide open spaces, creeks and rills, cutting across unexpected places, few buildings of any pretensions; not a sewer anywhere, surface drainage with a shallow, uncovered steam carrying off the refuse to the Potomac."[79]

Harriet Martineau, a young British traveler, was shocked by the sight of such "sordid…enclosures and houses" on the "very verge" of the seat of government. Staying for five weeks in a boardinghouse, she found the city to be "unlike any other that was ever seen,—straggling out hither and thither,—with a small house or two, a quarter of a mile from any other; so that in making calls 'in the city,' we had to cross ditches and stiles, and walk alternatively on grass and pavements, and strike across a field to reach a street."[80]

For the elite, Washington was slowly coming of age. Gas lanterns lined the streets, illuminating the city at night. Horse-drawn trolleys ran to and from the major social and political hubs, connecting senators and congressmen, journalists and cabinet ministers and, of course, wives and mistresses. But

An early rendering of the Capitol in Washington, D.C. *Library of Congress.*

for the less fortunate, life in the nation's capital was nothing grand. Some 4,696 slaves lived and worked in the district, accompanied by 8,361 free African Americans who also called Washington their home.[81]

"While we regard slavery in any part of our country as a flagrant violation of justice," the delegates at the Harrisburg meeting resolved, "we contemplate, with special regret and abhorrence its existence in that District," which they considered "the very inner court of freedom's temples....If any spot on earth, slavery should be known but as the curse of other lands and the disgrace of other times—should be heard of only in the traveller's tale and seen only on the historian's page...that spot is the District of Columbia."

They were outraged that thousands of "human beings, unaccused of any crime which could forfeit liberty, are held in the condition of 'chattels personal,' destitute of any acknowledged and protected rights, liable to all the wrongs and outrages which avarice, cruelty, or lust can suggest and arbitrary power can inflict, are consigned to the degradation which is inseparable from slavery." Slavery in the District differed from that in "the worst slave region" in the Deep South "only in the degree of severity with which it is administered."

But the great and crying abomination to which we would invite particular intention is the traffic in human flesh, which is actively and extensively carried on in the District, and between it and the several slaveholding states....The District is in truth, what it has been so often and justly styled, THE SLAVE MARKET of America. It has its established slave factories, where for 400 dollars a year, men are licensed "to trade or traffic in slaves for profit…" and where the victims of oppression are congregated from adjoining states like cattle at a fair, and purchases from various sections of the Union resort to procure "stock" for their plantations, or "servants" for other purposes. Even members of Congress and secretaries of state, are said to have sometimes availed themselves of the convenience afforded…to purchase slaves in this national slave mart.[82]

Washington, for many reasons, was ripe with symbolism. For abolitionists, not only was it the nation's capital, but it was also legislated directly by Congress. If they could convince Congress to abolish slavery there, it would be a crushing blow to proslavery forces everywhere. To fellow abolitionists in Massachusetts, the District represented "THE KEY OF SLAVERY. And when we have gained this Gibraltar," they proclaimed at an 1846 meeting, "we shall need no prophet to promise us the whole land."[83]

Doggedly, abolitionist meetings throughout the North returned to Washington as a central theme. In 1835, Dr. Reuben Crandall of New York, a physician and botanist, was arrested in Georgetown (part of the District) because he was carrying abolitionist publications. "It is said to have been with the utmost difficulty that the civil authorities saved him from being murdered on his way to the prison," cried abolitionists at a May 1836 meeting of the American Anti-Slavery Society in New York City. "Without having violated any law of the District, or of the United States, he was incarcerated from that time till the month of April." Charged with circulating "incendiary publications," Dr. Crandall was one of the first victims of a growing southern fear of slave revolts inspired by antislavery rhetoric.

Crandall was acquitted, but the damage had been done. Abolitionists seethed at the violation of his personal rights.

We charge it upon slavery, that in the 60th year of American independence, and the 48th of the Constitution, a citizen of a free state cannot safely pursue his business or pleasure, in the ten miles square, under the exclusive legislation of Congress. In that District has an honorable and inoffensive citizen of New-York been mobbed, and immured nine months

An abolitionist poster decrying the presence of slavery in the nation's capital. *Library of Congress.*

in an unwholesome dungeon, for presuming to interfere, in a moral and constitutional manner, with the sin and curse of traffic in human flesh! And yet abolitionists are asked, "How is slavery in the District a grievance to you?"[84]

The Harrisburg convention wrapped up on February 3, 1837, with a stirring declaration, defining both its purpose and future means. "If slavery be evil in its nature, and destructive in its tendencies," argued the committee of delegates charged with crafting a public statement, "if it involves an open and palpable violation of the laws of God, and of the duties of man toward his fellow; if the testimony of the whole civilized and even of the barbarian world is against it; and if we are implicated in its existence, as citizens of the United States…then we are called upon, by every principle which can animate us to virtuous action, to lift up our voices in behalf of its oppressed victims, and to cry aloud against a practice which violates the inherent rights of man."

How exactly the delegates planned to do so, they proceeded to outline:

And to do this more effectually, it becomes us to organize Anti-Slavery Societies over the length and breadth of the land; to use our talents and our means in diffusing information on this vitally interesting subject;—to publish and circulate facts, showing the enormities of the system;—to pour our petitions into the halls of Congress, praying for the abolition of slavery in the District of Columbia, and for the extinction of the domestic slave trade. Our object is to promote free discussion on the subject—to agitate it unceasingly until its dark and hideous features are brought to the surface, and placed in the view of every man, woman and child in the nation. We are convinced that the system requires only to be seen in its true light…to be abhorred.[85]

Placing slavery into its "true light" required overwhelming the nation with a tour de force of antislavery orators, newspapers, moralistic tracts and pamphlets. A new generation of northerners, with little or no firsthand experience with slavery, would need to realize the extent of its evils.

CHAPTER 3

"OF ONE BLOOD"

THE ADAMS COUNTY ANTI-SLAVERY SOCIETY

A dams County abolitionists were a diverse lot. For decades, Quakers in northern Adams County had been stalwarts of the antislavery cause.[86] In the town of Gettysburg, newspaper editor Robert W. Middleton and Pennsylvania College professor William Reynolds were anchors of support. A bustling African American community, which traced its existence back to the founding of the town, braved slave catchers and hostile sentiments. African American men such as Basil Biggs and Jack Hopkins put in extra hours on top of their day jobs to help freedom seekers reach safety. A mile to the southeast of Gettysburg, a Scotch-Irish Presbyterian, James McAllister, was a famous conductor on the Underground Railroad. To his southeast, in neighboring Mount Joy Township, a community of dedicated social activists helped propel the antislavery movement in Adams County to be one of the most extensive and active networks in the commonwealth.

Although the antislavery movement was rooted in faith, practicality required men and women who would translate that belief into tangible action. Who would collect signatures, write appeals, speak out and bring together discordant abolitionists in the pursuit of the greater cause?

For abolitionists in Adams County, that man was Adam Wert. Correspondents as distant as Philadelphia recognized him as the ideal point of contact to reach the myriad abolitionists living in Adams County. In terms of abolitionist activity, Adams County ranks among the most prolific counties in Pennsylvania—due in no small part to a heavy Quaker population in the northern tier of the county. However, members of other sects—Lutherans, Baptists, Presbyterians and Methodists—also worked actively in the reforms of the day.

Wert was a farmer who lived just two miles southeast of Gettysburg, in Mount Joy Township near White's Run. A "fine German scholar" who spoke and read "the choicest gems of a rich German literature," Wert supplemented his farming income by schoolteaching. At heart, however, he was a reformer. "Any one could touch Adam Wert if he gave out a hard luck story," his son recalled years later. "Early in life he had started out to be a philanthropist and a friend to humanity's downtrodden classes....He was, for a generation of darkling opposition, the staunch, uncompromising backbone of Adams county Abolitionism."[87]

On November 25, 1835, a "meeting of citizens" was held in Mount Joy Township. Two of Wert's neighbors ran the meeting—William Young was called to the chair, and Hezekiah Houghtelin Jr. was named secretary of the meeting. After Young and Houghtelin were installed, Adam Wert stood up and read seven resolutions, which were "adopted without a dissenting voice." The resolutions declared that "the existence of Slavery in the U. States is a moral and political evil, at variance with the principles of the Declaration of Independence, and a deep stain upon our National Character." The next two resolutions noted that "Congress possesses the Constitutional power to abolish Slavery in the District of Columbia," adding "that Congress ought to exercise this power without any further delay." The resolutions were then published in the *Gettysburg Star & Republican Banner.* The paper's editor, Robert W. Middleton, offered space for proponents of colonization as well as abolitionists and counted himself among the group of abolitionists.[88]

Nearly seven months later, on July 4, 1836, Wert served as secretary at a meeting at James McAllister's mill, just southeast of Gettysburg along the Baltimore Pike. There, he and other abolitionists adopted fourteen antislavery resolutions. Leading with the statement "[t]hat we receive as a Divine truth the declaration made by St. Paul at Athens…that 'God hath made of *one blood* all nations of men,'" the Adams Countians asserted that slavery was a moral evil. Other resolutions included:

> *4. Resolved, That, if liberty is the right of all men, no human being can be rightfully held in slavery.*
> *5. Resolved, That we cannot agree with those who profess to be opposed to slavery in the abstract, and who at the same time can find many excuses for slavery in practice; because, in our view, the whole evil of slavery consists in*

James McAllister, host of the July 4, 1836 meeting of the Adams County Anti-Slavery Society and a prominent "conductor" on the Underground Railroad in Gettysburg. *J. Howard Wert Gettysburg Collection.*

the practice of it, the discontinuance of which would be a complete removal of the evil.

6. Resolved, "That with a firm reliance on the protection of Divine Providence," we will make a diligent use of all proper means to procure the abolition of slavery....

14. Resolved, That although we may be denounced, for our efforts in the cause of human rights, by office-holding and office seeking politicians, and even by men wearing clerical robes, we will not be "afraid of their terror," but, disregarding their denunciations, we will continue to open our mouths for the dumb, and to plead the cause of the oppressed and of those who have none to help them, humbly believing, that, if we do unto others as we wish that they would do unto us, we shall have the approbation of Him who will render to every man, according to his works, and whose approbation will be a full remuneration for the loss of this world's favor.[89]

Wert hosted their next meeting—held on Constitution Day, September 17, 1836—at the small village of Two Taverns, a few miles southeast of Gettysburg near his home on the Baltimore Pike (a mile farther down from McAllister). Wert again stood up and offered fourteen resolutions—similar although slightly altered from their July meeting—in which he emphasized the Golden Rule. "The holding or selling of human beings, as property," Wert declared, "*is not* doing unto others as we wish that they should do unto us; and, therefore, the institution of Slavery is a direct and constant violation of that grand rule of human conduct, which is the essence of the Divine law." Others followed:

> *5. "We ought to obey God rather than man." Under every possible combination of circumstances, there is one safe course, and one only, and that is TO DO RIGHT—to obey God's command—and to trust Him with all the consequences. Therefore, discarding the fear of man…relying upon his Divine promise…we will employ our moral influence, and our political power, to "RELIEVE THE OPPRESSED," and to support the sacred cause of Human Rights.…*
>
> *9. It cannot reasonably be expected that Republican principles will become predominant in our world, until* professed *Republicans shall recognize by their* actions *the first principle of Republicanism: "ALL MEN ARE CREATED EQUAL."*

The meeting concluded by appointing a committee to arrange "a time and place for the holding of [an] *Anti-Slavery County Meeting.*"[90]

The next meeting, held at the courthouse in Gettysburg in December 1836, was interrupted by anti-abolition protestors, who hurled a variety of projectiles at the abolitionist orators, including eggs and even a dead cat. Nevertheless, they regrouped and formally organized as the Adams County Anti-Slavery Society.[91] McAllister was elected president, and Joel Wierman and Adam Wert were both elected vice presidents. Signers of their organizational charter included Quaker William Wright and *Star* editor Robert Middleton.[92] When the group chose delegates to go to the 1837 Harrisburg convention, Wierman, Middleton and Wert were among those chosen.[93]

Over the coming months, it became increasingly clear that Wert was the main organizational link between the Quaker farmers of northern Adams County and the abolitionists clustered in Gettysburg and to the southeast. "Adam Wert was the mainspring of the whole movement," recalled his son. "He would spend days, even weeks, going from house to house, setting up the machinery for a meeting he had planned. While manipulating the hidden springs he always endeavored to escape the appearance of undue prominence and to have the official places filled as far as practicable by others."[94]

When the group failed to meet as expected on July 4, 1837, Wert found himself soothing injured feelings. "I deeply regret that the fourth of the last Month passed by without our holding a meeting," wrote Joel Wierman. "I think the times call for an increase of energetic action." Wierman urged Wert, who seemed somewhat pessimistic over the future of the society, that "[s]uch of the Members as I have conversed with are of the same opinion & anxious that we should get together as soon as possible. I hope thee will take it upon thee to see the other members of the committee & if they can agree to it, call the members together by the twelf [*sic*] or nineteenth of this Month."[95] Wert took action and, at the next meeting, held on December 2, 1837, in Gettysburg, offered an amendment to the society's constitution, changing the structure of how meetings were "appointed" and arranged (one of Wierman's complaints in his August 6 letter). Wert then offered a resolution concerning the use of slave-produced products:

> *Whereas, the most odious system of human oppression—American Slavery—derives its most efficient support from the purchase of the produce of Slave-Labor by those who are not slave-holders, therefore, Resolved, that from and after the fourth day of July next, the members of this Society will not purchase any article of Merchandise which shall have been produced by the labor of American slaves.*[96]

Wert was following a long-practiced tradition of boycotting slave-produced goods. "Free men," wrote one British abolitionist, "must…prefer Free Produce—they must, upon reflection go a step further" and experience "some repugnance" to being "fed and clothed" by "the productions of Slavery."[97] "I hold this duty of abstinence to be the imperative duty of the moral abolitionist," one pamphleteer from Massachusetts had declared in 1835. "He who sees the tears of the slave on his cotton, or finds his blood in his sugar," should "religiously abstain" from those products.[98]

Within days of the December 2 meeting, William Reynolds, a member who was a professor at Pennsylvania College (later Gettysburg College), became aware that another antislavery convention was to be held in Harrisburg in January 1838. Faced with the task of appointing delegates, Reynolds scurried off a letter addressed to "Mr Adam Wert Mountjoy Township in haste," writing, "Shall the Abolitionists of Adams County be represented in that Convention? As to the question…I believe we are unanimously in favor of it." Reynolds noted, "Justice to ourselves demands that we should be, for there is not, in all probability, a county in the state where a stronger antislavery feeling exists."[99] Wert concurred and helped organize just such a meeting on December 30, at which eight delegates were appointed, including Middleton, Wright and Wierman.[100]

ON OCCASION, THE SOCIETY hosted abolitionist orators at public lectures in an attempt to sway local minds. In the late 1830s, James Miller McKim was nearly mobbed on the courthouse steps, as was Vermont's Jonathan Blanchard, another abolitionist lecturer. In December 1836, Blanchard had met a frosty reception in Carlisle, where a "large and respectable meeting of the citizens" requested him "not to deliver the discourse he intends to deliver in the Presb[yteria]n Church[.]" Like many other towns, they were wary of how southern neighbors, businessmen and relatives would react. "[T]he Subject of Abolition is one which carries with it…elements of excitement," they resolved, adding that it would produce "more evil than good consequences."[101] A few months later, in March 1837, Blanchard journeyed to Gettysburg, where he endured insults and a pelting of rotten eggs and stones. Speaking three times in one week at the Adams County Courthouse, Blanchard was met in debate by the town's most prominent citizens, who all declared abolition to be more destructive than helpful. Abolitionists, one prominent local declared, would precipitate a dissolution of the Union. In response, Blanchard declared that "[t]he South will never secede," for to do so, "she must lose immensely in profit, comfort and safety."[102]

One of Blanchard's lectures was interrupted by William McLean and his son Moses. William, a former judge, had made a name for himself by signing numerous warrants for the removal of fugitive slaves during the 1820s and early 1830s. His son Moses, himself now a judge, bellowed, "We have no slaves here, why come here to disturb our borough with discussion of slavery?" Blanchard's voice was drowned out by a sudden concourse of angry voices, and rotten eggs pelted his clothes (something he already was quite used to). Had it not been for the intervention of prominent locals, Blanchard feared the "mob, encouraged by elder and Judge McLean…would have injured me."[103] An irate Thaddeus Stevens returned to Gettysburg on Friday, March 17, to offer a resolution "asserting the right of *Free Discussion* upon any subject, and condemning all attempts to suppress the same or putting it down by mobs." Sizing up the crowd, Stevens declared, "A man comes to speak for *universal liberty*, him you answer with violence and rotten eggs! Shame! Shame!! SHAME!!! What freeman

Left: Jonathan Blanchard embarked upon a controversial 1837 tour of South Central Pennsylvania. His lecturing on abolition was generally unpopular and often met with violence. *Wheaton College Archives and Special Collections.*

Right: A rendering of a young Frederick Douglass during his early years of antislavery activism. *National Portrait Gallery, Smithsonian Institution.*

does not feel himself covered all over with burning blushes, to find himself surrounded by SUCH freemen?"[104]

One observer remembered that Stevens

> *was calm, deliberate, impressive, and the excited crowd listened with earnest attention....Warming gradually with his subject, he enforced the right of free discussion on all subjects with a power and an eloquence which his audience had never heard. The sacred rights of American citizenship, secured by constitutional guarantees, were defended by a master hand. In turn he used persuasion, entreaty, argument, wit, and sarcasm, until finally, turning to his old neighbors and friends, he appealed to their sense of honor and justice, to their individual reputation and the reputation of their community, as deeply involved in their contemplated proceedings; and when he took his seat the [anti-abolition] resolutions, which had been previously adopted without a dissenting voice, found no one bold enough to advocate their passage. On the contrary, a new set of resolutions were introduced and passed with singular unanimity, affirming the right of free discussion and inviting this early anti-slavery missionary to continue his labors.*[105]

The danger was even greater for black lecturers. Frederick Douglass, an escaped slave who rose to fame as an abolitionist lecturer, lived in constant fear of being kidnapped and returned to bondage. Fellow abolitionists warned him not to attend meetings "along the borders of" Pennsylvania, and Douglass himself "felt that I was rubbing against my prison wall, and could not go any further." In the early 1840s, Douglass's visit to Gettysburg put his life and liberty in dire danger. "[A]s I came along the vales and hills of Gettysburg," he later recalled, "my good friends, the anti-slavery people along there warned me to remain in the house during the day-time, and travel in the night, lest I should be kidnapped, and carried over into Maryland."[106]

Abby Kelley, a noted abolitionist lecturer who braved largely hostile crowds in Gettysburg. *Library of Congress.*

In 1845, James Miller McKim arranged for Abby Kelley, a noted Quaker abolitionist from Massachusetts, to lecture in Gettysburg. McKim was well aware of the extensive network of abolitionists in Adams County, writing to Adam Wert:

> *You will have seen by the* [Pennsylvania] *"Freeman"* [newspaper] *that Miss Abby Kelly & company are journey-ing toward Adams County.… They will probably be with you in a fortnight…perhaps sooner. I am anxious that they should have a good house & fair hearing in Gettysburg, and write with the hope of securing your friends offices towards this end. Will you not repair at once to Gettysburg and confirm with the friends there as to the best mode of getting our friends a good hearing?*[107]

Upon reaching Gettysburg, Kelley's manager, Benjamin S. Jones, was met with a cool response. Unable to obtain lodging, he lamented that "the professed abolitionists here are not the kind to act efficiently," writing to Wert, "From what I have heard of you, you are the one to see that things go right.…Remember the responsibility rests on you for no one else will attend to it." Jones believed "the folks here are afraid of the women" and would not listen to Kelley due to her gender.[108] Even nine years after the Anti-Slavery Society's inception, Gettysburg was still no cradle for abolitionism.

LOCALLY, THE SOCIETY FOUND its most effective tactic was that of quiet intimidation. With some 21,334 residents recorded at the 1830 census, Adams Countians lived mostly in small towns and farming communities.[109] If someone cooperated with slave catchers or blew the whistle on a fugitive slave stowed away nearby, word would spread quickly among the extensive and oftentimes high-placed Anti-Slavery Society members. Adams County millers James McAllister and Jesse Cook, both active Underground Railroad conductors, might refuse service to whistleblowing farmers who needed their grain milled for market. Thaddeus Stevens, along with members of the Wierman and Wert families, served on the board of the Gettysburg Bank. According to other abolitionists, Stevens and those serving on the board used threats of financial pressure, intimating that difficulties in procuring future loans might befall anyone who colluded with slave catchers or authorities.[110]

Although Stevens himself was not a member of the Anti-Slavery Society, he was closely linked with Middleton, who was a regular attendee and crucial supporter of the society. For years, Stevens had been affiliated with many of the county's leading abolitionists. He had served with Adam Wert on the town council; had represented various members of the McAllister, Wierman and Wright clans as a lawyer; and, in 1835, had jointly purchased land with the Wiermans near York Springs. In western Adams County, the superintendent of his Caledonia Iron Works, William Hammett, was well known to Franklin County "agents" who ushered freedom seekers along the spine of South Mountain to Caledonia. Farther to the east, in Fairfield, Stevens was widely suspected by locals there of involvement on the Underground. The furnace master's house at Maria Furnace, defunct by the late 1830s, was known for having an emergency exit accessible through the attic. Another house he owned near Fairfield was reputed to have a false wall in the basement, ideal for concealing runaways. Stevens was also unafraid of using positions of power to further his antislavery sentiments. In 1839, Stevens, a member of the Gettysburg School Board, arranged for the dismissal of William McLean as a schoolteacher after he spoke out against abolitionists at a public meeting in Gettysburg.[111]

Events out of their control in Washington, however, forced the Adams Countians to add new tactics to their repertoire. As abolitionists throughout the North became more vocal, southerners became defensive. Petitions for the abolition of slavery found their way to Congress, only to be tabled and subsequently ignored with regularity. One stalwart in presenting these petitions, no matter their content, was John Quincy Adams, the sixth president of the United States (1825–29). After he was defeated for reelection

Thaddeus Stevens, 1838. This engraving, based on a painting by Jacob Eichholtz, depicts Stevens in front of Pennsylvania College (now Gettysburg College). As Gettysburg's state representative, Stevens helped to obtain the college's charter. However, his antislavery views made him a controversial figure, and he relocated to Lancaster in 1842. *Library of Congress.*

in 1828, Adams was elected by his neighbors to a Massachusetts House seat, making him the first president to hold office after his presidency.

Adams doggedly believed in the right of free speech, namely the right of citizens to petition their government. Stubbornly, Adams continued to present abolition petitions, despite heated backlash from his colleagues, both North and South. On May 25, 1836, a combination of southern congressmen and their northern allies changed the rules of the House, stating that "for the purpose of arresting agitation, and restoring tranquility to the public mind…all petitions, memorials, resolutions, propositions, or papers relating in any way to the subject of slavery, or the abolition of slavery," would be tabled "without either being printed or referred… and that no further action whatever be had upon them."

Former president John Quincy Adams sparked the debate over the "Gag Rule" as a congressman in the 1830s. *Library of Congress.*

The former president was irate. His protest soon became a sensation, as Adams harangued the Speaker all the while pointing out that "a slaveholding Speaker occupied the chair." Defying repeated calls to come to "order" and commands to take his seat, the former president combatively fought the motion to a pulse, culminating in the famous line, "Mr. Speaker, am I gagged, or not?"

Ultimately, the motion passed, but thanks to Adams's impassioned attack, it became known as the odious "gag rule." For many abolitionists, it was the proof they needed to satisfy themselves that the government was run by a slaveholders' oligarchy, commonly referred to as "the slave power." Adams was correct in saying that the "gag rule" was "in direct violation of the Constitution of the United States, of the rules of the House, and of the rights of my constituents."[112] Few events did more to energize the antislavery movement.

Throughout the North, the "gag rule" and its effects were the most frequent topic of discussion. Like their compatriots throughout New England and the Midwest, the abolitionists of Adams County drafted and adopted several resolutions, declaring that free speech was "a right which no human power can take away." The "right of Free Discussion," they continued, "is Necessary and essential to the maintenance & security of our other rights and that without this other rights would be of little value." So, too, was the right to petition, which they deemed "a sacred & Inalienable right & guaranteed to us by the Constitution of the United States." The "gag rule" was nothing more than "an unwarrantable assumption of power by the Servants of the people against which we protest."[113]

THE ADAMS COUNTIANS WERE in tune with abolitionists throughout the North. Collectively, they emphasized free speech as quintessential to revealing the evils of slavery. "As for all the clamor, and violence, and threats, which our cause has called forth, they only convince us, that we have hit the nail upon the head," abolitionists in New York declared. "[T]hese things prove to us that we are right; and if we are not encountered by a gag law, if the press is not muzzled, and the right of free speech is allowed us, the truth will go far and wide, its power will be felt throughout the land, and slavery will die."[114] A convention of New Englanders was convinced that the "same lawless power, which binds the colored man to slavery, calls for a gag to be put in our mouths. Give it that, and how long before it will put a yoke upon our necks?" The "gag rule" was bound to "make the freemen of the North slaves....The grand question at issue now is, whether the South have a right to hold us of the North in subjection."[115]

Asserting their right to free speech, within a few months the Adams Countians were busy gathering signatures and sending petitions to their congressmen. Adam Wert once more took a leading role, coordinating the petitions and sending them to legislators under his name. In February 1837, Wert received a reply from lame duck congressman George Chambers, who informed Wert that he had presented his "memorial requesting the abolition of slavery & the slave trade in the District of Columbia." Wert found a sympathetic ear in Chambers, who lamented the general apathy "not only tolerating slavery in the District, but allowing it to be the great Slave Market of the United States; yet," he wrote pessimistically, "nothing will be done by the present Congress, whether to afford any protection to the coloured population of the District, or abolish the abominable institution of trafficking in human beings, under circumstances of oppression & cruelty."[116] In August 1837, Joel Wierman wrote Wert to say that he had "many petitions on hand, More than I can attend to, & I hope some thing will be done to put them in circulation."[117]

The subjects of their petitions, however, soon came to include a new specter looming heavily on the political stage. For some time, Benjamin Lundy and other abolitionists had been carefully monitoring the developments along the United States' southwestern border. The Mexican government had previously welcomed American settlers in the region known as Texas, intending that the American frontiersmen would serve as a buffer between the Rio Grande and raiding Comanches, who controlled a vast swath of the Great Plains to the north. Their amicable arrangement deteriorated, however, with the ascension of Mexican leader Santa Anna, who outlawed slavery in Mexico. When Texans refused to obey the new Mexican statutes, Santa Anna led a famous military expedition, which resulted in his own capture.

With Texas independence accomplished in 1836, abolitionists feared and rightly expected the proslavery settlers to apply for statehood. In Texas, they saw another proving ground for America to live up to the doctrine of the Declaration of Independence. If Texas was to be annexed as a state (or possibly multiple states, increasing the number of slave senators), "the whole slave system" would be "invigorated," the Massachusetts Anti-Slavery Society anticipated, "because it opens an immense territory, new and fertile, to the traffickers in human flesh, and of course greatly enhances the market value of 'slaves and souls of men.'" It also threatened to disrupt the balance of slave and free state senators in Washington—which abolitionists referred to as "a dangerous augmentation of political power…into the hands of a slaveholding aristocracy more imperious and rapacious than all the aristocracies of the old world *en masse*." They held this "slavocracy" responsible for systematically stifling the "freedom of speech and of the press, the rights of conscience, personal protection…the unobstructed and impartial circulation of the Bible, true gospel fidelity in preaching, and the benefits of education for all classes."[118]

Benjamin Lundy was among the first to sound the alarm, publishing a work titled *The War in Texas* in 1836. Written in the midst of the conflict, Lundy's lengthy, meandering subtitle said it all—he billed his book as a "review of [the] facts and circumstances, showing that this contest is the result of a long premeditated CRUSADE AGAINST THE GOVERNMENT, set on foot by *Slaveholders, Land Speculators, &c.* with the view of Re-Establishing, Extending, and Perpetuating the system of SLAVERY AND THE SLAVE TRADE in the Republic of Mexico." Although many "have been induced to believe that the inhabitants of Texas were engaged in a legitimate contest for the maintenance of the sacred principles of Liberty, and the natural, inalienable Rights of Man," this was far from the truth, Lundy wrote. The "immediate cause and the leading object of this contest originated in a settled design," he claimed, "among the slaveholders of this country…to wrest the large and valuable territory of Texas from the Mexican Republic, in order to re-establish the SYSTEM OF SLAVERY; to open a vast and profitable SLAVEMARKET therein; and, ultimately, to annex it to the United States."

With Andrew Jackson in the presidential chair, the Quaker despaired that "[t]he Slaveholding Interest is now paramount in the Executive branch… and its influence operates, indirectly, yet powerfully, through that medium, in favor of this Grand Scheme of Oppression and Tyrannical Usurpation." Would Congress "join hands" with Jackson "and lend its aid to this most unwarrantable, aggressive attempt" to introduce another slave state into the Union? The decision of Congress on "this unhallowed scheme," he wrote, "will depend on the VOICE OF THE PEOPLE, expressed in their primary assemblies, by their petitions, and through the ballot boxes."[119] It was a call to action for his readers and fellow abolitionists throughout the country.

Lundy's devoted following of friends and relatives in York Springs needed little persuasion to join his cause. In 1837, abolitionists throughout Adams County signed a petition protesting the admission of Texas. The petition, sent to Congressman Daniel Sheffer, Chambers's successor, was "signed by Adam Wert and sixty seven other voters of Adam[s] County." Sheffer presented the petition in January 1838, but due to the gag rule, it was "overruled by some distant member asking it to be laid on the table." However, he consolingly wrote to Adam Wert: "When the time comes that any member will move the admission of Texas into the Union then we can get our petitions before a committee."[120]

In this waiting game, Sheffer was effusively apologetic, writing to Wert on May 14 with a lengthy excuse for the delay, followed by the caveat: "Abolition petitions particularly don't find favour or indulgence with the Southerners— All is quiet as regards to Texas.…I am satisfied that we have Territory enough in that quarter without more."[121] Although a Democrat, Sheffer had reason to placate Wert and his vocal antislavery constituency—he was running for reelection in 1838 (a race he would ultimately lose).

To this point, the Adams Countians were keenly aware of the importance of their votes. In other states, the Liberty Party—a third party promoting the abolition of slavery—had been fingered as a spoiler in state and national elections. Although only polling a few percentage points, in tight races between Whigs and Democrats, the Liberty Party's small margin became quite noticeable. With "the approaching election for Senator in our state Legislature," Allen Robinette, a Latimore township Quaker, took up his pen to write to Adam Wert. The election "is exciting some interest and inquiry by the Abolitionists here." Discussing the candidates, Robinette thought both the Whig and the Democrat "bitterly opposed to us, & the cause of the Oppressed, [and] Consequently alike unworthy [of] the suffrages of freemen, it becomes therefore an important inquiry whether Abolitionists can consistently vote for either—my present impression is that if they are Equally Violent in their Opposition to Anti slavery principles, it would be wrong for us to vote for either, but if one or the other should be less violent in their Opposition to us, then, I think of two evils, we should choose the least[.]"[122]

As a testament to their political influence, the Adams Countians received sympathetic responses from all three congressmen who represented Adams County between 1836 and 1842. In 1840, Whig James Cooper (Sheffer's successor) responded to Wert's petition for the "immediate termination of slavery and the Slave trade in the District of Columbia." Cooper, who had spoken out against abolitionist agitation in the past, struck a sympathetic note in his letter to Wert: "God grant that the day may soon come when this subject will be more respected. Be assured that I will not neglect to present the petition which you have forwarded to me at the very first moment that it is possible for me to do so."[123] A similar response came the following year to a petition "to repeal all laws in the District of Columbia which are inconsistent with the Declaration of Independence."[124] Ever persistent, another petition reached Cooper's desk in early 1842. Cooper reminded Wert of the gag rule, explaining that "under the rule," the petition was "laid upon the table. This is the case with all petitions of this kind." He did, however, express hope "that it will be repealed when a motion now lying on the table can be got up in order."[125]

In the meantime, President John Tyler had pursued a vigorous strategy to bring Texas into the Union. Together with his newly named secretary of state, John C. Calhoun, Tyler drew up a treaty to annex Texas in April 1844. Just southeast of Gettysburg, miller James McAllister learned of the developments via his subscription to *The Madisonian*, a Washington paper. Disgusted, McAllister wrote Wert of the "official announcement that the President of the United States, has actually signed a Treaty for the Annexation of Texas." Although McAllister had expected the worst, he was still shocked at what he viewed as a "high-handed measure.... [N]ow that the act is consummated, we cannot but contemplate with amazement an assumption of authority so bold, and one involving consequences as momentous[.]" That a proslavery president could enter into a treaty "on his own mere notion with a foreign Government" to assume "as large as the entire kingdom of France" was contemptible in McAllister's eye. Imbued with the combative spirit of reform, he added: "The senate has not yet ratified the Treaty, there is therefore yet Hope[.]"[126] Ultimately, the treaty would be ratified, and Texas became part of the Union.

YEARS LATER, ABOLITIONISTS WOULD have a congressman of their own stock. Edward McPherson was born in Gettysburg on July 31, 1830, and graduated from Pennsylvania College in 1848. As a McPherson, Edward was a member of one of Gettysburg's most prominent families. His paternal grandfather, Colonel Robert McPherson, was noted for his military service and held the offices of auditor, commissioner, sheriff and assemblyman during the latter half of the eighteenth century. The colonel also owned eleven slaves in 1783, and at least two of his sons (Edward's uncles) followed suit. William McPherson, the eldest, owned slaves and in 1805 advertised for the return of "a Negro servant for years, named *Jim*, about 19 years of age[.]" In 1818, he again advertised for a runaway slave named Jack Kelley, a fifty-year-old man who was, according to McPherson's advertisement, "a slave for life[.]" William's brother Robert also owned slaves and in 1810 sought to sell an "active, healthy *Young Negro Man*, who has about eight years to serve."[127]

Edward, however, charted a different path. He studied law under Thaddeus Stevens and absorbed more than law books during his tutelage. They remained close political allies until Stevens's death in 1868. McPherson, in the meantime, won a congressional seat encompassing much of Adams and Franklin Counties in 1858 and was reelected in 1860. When the war broke out, Adams County abolitionists cheered as McPherson delivered a fiery speech on the House floor titled "The Disunion Conspiracy." In it, he alleged that southerners had manipulated the Democratic Party, laws and policies to protect slavery. "On all questions affecting slavery," he cried, "they treat the Constitution with violence; stretching it far beyond its letter or spirit." McPherson was a proponent of the "slave power" theory, which argued the southern "slavocracy" was manipulating the arms of the federal government to protect slavery before republican values—a line of thought articulated earlier by Benjamin Lundy during the Texas controversy.[128]

ADAMS COUNTY'S LARGE AFRICAN American population pulled its share as well. Evidence indicates that most of the work of "practical abolition"—leading fugitives from one home to another—was done by local blacks. Although the Anti-Slavery Society apparently had no black members, Adams County blacks organized on their own. Members of St. Paul's African Methodist Episcopal Church, on the corner of Breckenridge and Washington Streets in Gettysburg, founded the Slave's Refuge Society, tasked with assisting "such of our brethren as shall come among us for the purpose of liberating themselves[.]" Founding members included James Cameron, Henry Butler,

Equal Rights to all—Exclusive Privilege to None.

No motto for Americans
  More comprehensive seems
Than this, inscribed upon our flag
  That in the sunlight gleams.
This principle of Liberty
  With her shall rise or fall,
Exclusive privilege to NONE,
  And "EQUAL RIGHT's to all."
The lordly aristocracy
  Repulse its light with scorn ;
But Tyranny's monopoly
  Of all its power is shorn.
When men, in God's own image, rise
  And at their country's call,
Assert and well defend the cause
  Of " EQUAL RIGHT's to all."
Nor birth, nor wealth, nor pride, have
  place
  Within the hallowed dome,
Where Liberty her laurel wears,
  And FREEMEN find their home.
For brightly gleams the characters
  Etched on our cherished scroll,
"Exclusive privilege to none,
  But EQUAL RIGHT's to all."
The poor man, honest in his toil,
  The rich with plenty blest,
Shall each hold Freedom's heritage.
  And Heaven shall grant the rest !
We'll cherish then our motto pure,
  Freedom of Mind ank Soul,—
"Exclusive privilege to none,
  But EQUAL RIGHT's to all.

Above: Jack Hopkins, the janitor of Pennsylvania College, used his contacts with local abolitionist families to help runaway slaves. *Special Collections, Gettysburg College.*

Left: "Equal Rights to All—Exclusive Privilege to None." One of the many poems clipped by Smith, it reflects her commitment to the egalitarian ideals most notably championed by her employer, Thaddeus Stevens. *J. Howard Wert Gettysburg Collection.*

James Jones, Henry Chiler and John Jones.[129] Given the history of black antislavery activism, the church's central role is hardly surprising. For over two centuries, black abolitionism had been built upon an "antiracist construction of Christianity," where African Americans emphasized the spiritual equality of slaves as a means of undermining slavery.[130] At nearby Pennsylvania College (later Gettysburg College), Jack Hopkins, a black janitor, cooperated with white students who formed a fraternity known as the Black Ducks. Hopkins and the students helped lead freedom seekers to and from different Underground stations.[131]

Some ten miles to the north, Edward and Annie Mathews lived on Yellow Hill in Quaker Valley. In the midst of friendly Quakers, they enjoyed the relative comfort of neighborly protection. Two of their sons, Samuel and Nelson, found work at the nearby farms of Hiram and Cyrus Griest, both

Lydia Hamilton Smith, an Adams County native, rose to national prominence as a confidant of Thaddeus Stevens. *J. Howard Wert Gettysburg Collection.*

Russell's Tavern, south of Biglerville, the 1815 birthplace of Lydia Hamilton Smith. Her working relationship with Stevens placed her in a crucial position to both influence and witness the destruction of slavery in the United States. *Photo by Stephen Kohler.*

Quaker abolitionists, cementing a key route on the Underground Railroad. From James McAllister's mill southeast of Gettysburg, Basil Biggs—a black veterinarian and tenant farmer residing near the town—led fugitive slaves on foot to the Mathews farmhouse on Yellow Hill. From there, Edward Mathews brought them to Cyrus Griest's farm, concealing the runaways in Griest's springhouse. A light tap on the Griests' bedroom window alerted Cyrus and his wife, Mary Ann, to their presence. The next morning, breakfast would be prepared and brought out to the springhouse. Later that evening, the freedom seekers would typically move on, either northeast to York Springs or north into Cumberland County.[132]

Lydia Hamilton Smith, an African American woman who lived most of her life outside Adams County, also made crucial contributions. Born in 1815 at Russell's Tavern, near Biglerville, Smith was a devout Catholic. While her mother worked as a servant at the tavern, her father was likely Enoch Hamilton, a white man who had married into the Russell family. During the 1830s, she worked at a Harrisburg hotel while Thaddeus Stevens served in the legislature. They soon met, and over the years, Smith became a close confidant of Stevens. After he relocated to Lancaster, he hired Smith as his housekeeper. Although the exact nature of their relationship has been widely speculated, Smith's religious commitment to antislavery principles and loyalty to a man who espoused them on the public stage remain clear. Among her personal possessions are religious wafers and clipped poems of antislavery poet laureate John Greenleaf Whittier.[133]

CHAPTER 4

"BY RELIGIOUS PROFESSION"

FRANKLIN COUNTY ABOLITIONISTS

S lave catchers abounded in Franklin County. The northerly extension of Virginia's Shenandoah Valley and Maryland's Cumberland Valley, it was as natural a route for freedom seekers as it was for those intent on profiting from their plight. Popular sentiment, too, tended to favor slaveholders. In April 1837, the Franklin County Courthouse played host to a "GREAT ANTI ABOLITION MEETING." Believing that abolitionists "not only endanger the purity and good order of our national councils, but tend to distract the tranquility of the country," the group of prominent citizens—headlined by former congressman George Chambers, the grandson of the town's founder—lamented "the existence of Slavery in any part of the world" but found "the doctrines and acts of the abolitionists" even more devastating. Abolition, they declared, was "at war with the true history of our colonial and national existence[.]" They argued that southern states would abolish slavery on their own, provided they were left alone.[134]

As early as 1827, religious leaders in Chambersburg had sought to encourage locals to join the American Colonization Society. However, leaders of that movement were generally more concerned with removing free blacks from northern soil than the well-being of the millions still in bondage. Colonization would remain a popular theme in Franklin County until the outbreak of the Civil War.[135] Abolition, however, excited great hostility. "The exertions of the Abolition Societies continue to produce bitter fruits," the *Franklin Repository* complained in May 1838. "They are Riots, Mobs, Arson and Murder…binding tighter and tighter the chains of the Slave, and engendering sentiments of hatred and disunion in the minds of his master!"[136]

Like in most of the antebellum North, anti-black sentiment was also a popular train of thought. The *Valley Spirit*, another Chambersburg paper, denounced "filthy, theiving [*sic*], whisky drinking negroes," arguing for their expulsion from Chambersburg. "If there were no such 'local habitations' provided for them they would take up their abode in other quarters and this neighborhood would get rid of their troublesome presence." In addition to drunkenness and theft, the paper accused Chambersburg's black residents of "licentious and blasphemous orgies," living in "a state of nudity" and carrying illnesses.[137] When Nathaniel Freeman, a free black, was sentenced to the state penitentiary for larceny, the paper mocked: "Freeman is no longer a free man, though we believe he is still a black man. Well, he had no business to meddle with other people's poor innocent sheep skins and beef hides, and it was perfectly right to send him were [*sic*] all bad n----rs go."[138]

Among poorer whites, competition for work drove anti-black sentiment. During the 1850 congressional election, Democrat James X. McLanahan ran on the promise that he "is in favor of supporting the poor white man in preference to the negro." If voters "do not wish your country overwhelmed with idle, lay negroes from Maryland, Virginia and other slave states vote for James X. McLanahan for Congress." Speaking to the "poor men who depend upon your daily labor to gain a living for yourselves and families," the Democratic *Valley Spirit* warned that "if the abolitionists get a sufficient number of members of Congress, they will abolish slavery, and then the Negroes will overrun the free States, and work for less wages and you will be compelled to work for the same or have nothing to do. Are you willing to work side by side with a negro, for ten cents a day? Are you willing to sleep in the same bed with him? Are you willing that the negro shall be the companion of your sons and daughters?" McLanahan won the seat.[139]

An 1853 notice declared that "five darkeys from Mercersburg, (one of them a female,) were committed in prison yesterday, charged with stealing bacon and chickens, and doing various other naughty things." Reporting the prison population to be "seventeen negroes and three white persons," the editors of the *Valley Spirit* argued that if "slavery were abolished in the South and the freed negroes were permitted to 'spread themselves' over the country, we should have about seven times seventeen to support in prison. God knows we have enough to provide for now; and having enough, it is not strange that our people have little feeling in common with abolitionists of the Smith and Stowe breed."[140]

For the most part, Franklin Countians—like most northerners—did not wish to be bothered by slavery. "Our subscribers do not own slaves, and it is therefore quite unnecessary to trouble them with a harangue about the sinfulness of retaining human beings in bondage," noted the editor of the *Valley Spirit* in 1852. "For our own part, we should be sorry to see the slaves of the South emancipated, without provision being made for sending them out of the country. We want no more free negroes in Pennsylvania. There are too many here now, eking out an existence as miserable as it is hopeless of amelioration. If they were all slaves to kind masters, they would be far better off than they are now."[141]

In part due to local sentiment, slave catchers were able to operate with high rates of success. They were often assisted by local constabulary, who sought the hefty rewards for themselves.[142] In the early 1830s, John Grove, a constable in Chambersburg, responded to an advertisement from a slaveholder in Winchester seeking two runaways. Grove offered to "assist in returning the fugitive for the promised sum." The slaveholder and Grove found the two men, but during their hearing (under an 1826 state law), the men denied their identities or even knowing the man who claimed to be their owner. Only courtroom theatrics could send them back into bondage. Reade Washington, counsel for the slaveholder, attempted just that. He turned his back to the men before "suddenly wheeling about" and shouting "Bob!"—one of the names testified by the slaveholder. Instinctively, one of the men replied, "Sir." This was all the evidence a Franklin County court needed to send the two men back with the slaveholder.[143]

Sam Davis, a runaway slave from Virginia, found himself followed into a shop by "two musket-bearing men," who proceeded to take him captive.[144] Even when caught kidnapping free blacks, slave catchers were seldom convicted. In 1851, Barnard Foltz and William B. Johnston were arrested for "unlawfully carrying away a little darkey from the free dirt of Pennsylvania," sneered the *Valley Spirit*, "with a view of reducing him to a state of servitude in Virginia." The pair merely received a slap on the wrist and were found not guilty. Many, including the anti-abolitionist editors at the *Valley Spirit*, scoffed at the charges. "The evidence, it would seem from the verdict, did not bear out the accusation."[145]

Hagerstown slave catchers "were frequent visitors to Chambersburg and even to Shippensburg," recalled one local. One of those men, Joe Price, "had a closely covered wagon, that was a familiar object in the streets of Chambersburg, and when it turned into a hotel yard, there was a general conviction that if there was not a 'darkey' inside, there soon would be."

Henry Freamer was another "Maryland kidnapper" who made frequent trips to Shippensburg. There, several locals concealed recaptured fugitives in a hotel until his arrival.[146]

Although many slave catchers came from the South, the Logan family, near Mount Alto, were homegrown slave catchers. Brothers Daniel and Hugh Logan were "both shrewd, quiet, resolute men, both strongly Southern in their sympathies, [and] both natural detectives." The name Logan was regarded with fear and apprehension among the county's black population.[147] Ironically, slave catchers and abolitionists were sometimes related by blood, and in one case, a pair of brothers personified the divide. Wagon maker Samuel Taylor of Leesburg, in western Cumberland County, was a well-known abolitionist, while his brother Barney was known as "a big man in the 'gang'" of slave catchers operating in the valley.[148]

Multiple accounts point to free blacks in Franklin County who worked with slave catchers.[149] Near Chambersburg, a black man named Joe Winters was widely suspected of tricking runaways into trusting him and then reporting their locations to local authorities or slave catchers for a monetary reward. Blacks cooperating with slave catchers were known as "handkerchiefheads."[150] If the claims against him were true, Winters appears to have acted independently. For several decades, slave catchers had been employing a favorite trick they called a "decoy negro." In 1837, slave catchers bragged that three runaways near Mercersburg were "housed by a decoy negro, who, the same afternoon, appraised [*sic*] some constables…of the fact."[151]

NEVERTHELESS, ANTISLAVERY SYMPATHIZERS REMAINED a quiet but impactful group in Franklin County. Many quietly operated Underground Railroad routes, a fact slaveholders in neighboring Maryland and nearby Virginia were well aware of. "I hereby forewarn all persons from harboring, hiring, or carrying off said Negroes at their peril," vowed one slave owner in a runaway ad published in the *Franklin Repository*.[152]

In his wanderings through Franklin County, abolitionist lecturer Jonathan Blanchard found many friends. "[W]e have just organized an Anti-Slavery Society at this place, under favorable auspices," he wrote from Quincy, a small town in eastern Franklin County. "Twenty-seven gave their names at first, but the list will immediately be almost indefinitely swelled; as the inhabitants of Quincy and vicinity are for the most part Abolitionists, many of them by religious profession."[153]

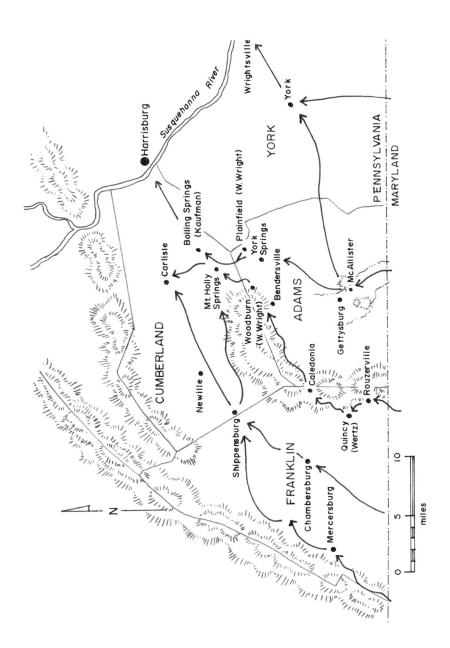

The Underground Railroad in South Central Pennsylvania. *Map by John Heiser.*

Among the abolitionists Blanchard likely would have met was Matthew Dobbin, a Gettysburg native who had left his hometown under financial difficulties. In Quincy, he boarded with the Wertz family while teaching school. The Wertzes' son, Hiram, enjoyed paging through Dobbin's subscription to *The National Era*, an abolitionist publication out of Washington. In the mid-1840s, Dobbin took young Hiram Wertz under his wing and showed him the workings of a local Underground Railroad route, setting Wertz on a lifelong path against slavery. The route Wertz inherited led from his father's barn eight miles north, along the slopes of South Mountain, to "Little Africa," home to some two dozen African American families and adjacent to Thaddeus Stevens's Caledonia Ironworks. "It would have been a sorrowful time for any one to have ventured into this neighborhood with the idea of attempting to arrest any fugitives," Wertz later recalled.[154]

To the north of Quincy, Black Gap (between Scotland and Fayetteville) offered safety to the fugitive. Standing six feet, six inches tall, Robert Black III owned a farm and general store and manned a post office along a road cleared by his grandfather, giving name to the small settlement. Whereas Dobbin and Wertz's line ran east into Adams County, Black's route ran north up the valley. Runaways typically arrived during the night, and Black would feed and shelter them until the following evening. Then, "they would be sent forward on horseback" northward, likely to Shippensburg, Boiling Springs or Carlisle.[155]

Near Black's Gap, "Crawford's Lane" referred to an easterly route passing through Fayetteville. There, Dr. Samuel Wylie Crawford, a Presbyterian minister, directed freedom seekers eastward, across the mountain to Caledonia. A graduate of the University of Pennsylvania, Crawford had dabbled in medicine but preferred theological studies. His strong religious background propelled him to work on the Underground Railroad.[156]

In Antrim township, in southern Franklin County, the mixed-race Anderson family was also involved. The family traced their lineage back to Robert Anderson, a Northern Irishman who had been involved in the transatlantic slave trade during the late 1700s. Apparently, the cruel trade was too much for Anderson to bear, and on his last trip, he proposed to an African woman on the voyage, promising her freedom if she accepted. One of their sons, Timothy Anderson, came to Antrim township, where he operated a farm. Timothy and his children offered shelter to freedom seekers, who were concealed in a "secret enclosure" in the family home.[157]

GENERALLY, THE RURAL COUNTRYSIDE was more conducive to abolitionism than urban areas such as Chambersburg. As the county seat, Chambersburg relied heavily on southern customers, travelers and clients. From the 1820s until the Civil War, editors of the town's main papers deplored abolition and spewed anti-black sentiment. Yet despite all the obstacles, Chambersburg was nevertheless home to an assortment of abolitionists who helped freedom seekers to safety and, in 1859, made their mark on the national stage.

James Lesley, a Philadelphia-born bank clerk, came to Chambersburg in 1845 to take the job of cashier at the town's main bank. Known as a "somewhat eccentric character," he was also regarded as "a man of high character, and a strong anti-slavery man at a time when it required courage to oppose the slave system." During his thirteen-year residency, Lesley's house on the southwest side of the square was a frequent haven for fugitive slaves.[158] George Cole, a free black, was also a participant. He famously became embroiled in a Cumberland County court trial as the man who led thirteen fugitive slaves north from Chambersburg.[159]

By far the most famous abolitionist resident of Chambersburg was Martin R. Delany. Born free in Charlestown, Virginia (modern-day West Virginia), his family had fled when it was revealed that Martin and his brothers were literate—a crime under Virginia state law. Spending his formative years in Chambersburg, Delany found that opportunities for education and advancement were slim. At age nineteen, he relocated to Pittsburgh, where he rose through the ranks of the city's budding African American community, emerging as a leading voice in the fight against slavery. Impressed by Delany, Frederick Douglass brought him on as co-editor of his antislavery serial the *North Star* from 1847 to 1849. However, ideological differences soon produced cracks in their relationship, and they parted ways. In the ensuing decades, the two were often at odds, Delany at times advocating for black immigration to South America or Africa. During the Civil War, Delany became the first black major to be commissioned in the Union army.[160]

Although not as widely known, a black barber named Henry Watson was an important figure in Chambersburg's antislavery community during the 1850s. Like John Peck had done previously in Carlisle, Watson established connections with local and national networks of abolitionists. In 1859, his position would bring him into close contact with one of the most controversial abolitionists in history.[161]

CHAPTER 5

"THE WINDOWS WERE CLOSED TO PREVENT DISCOVERY"

YORK COUNTY ABOLITIONISTS

L ike their neighbors, abolitionists in York County faced daunting proslavery and pro-southern sentiment. The county's southern border with Maryland precipitated trade and intermarriage with slaveholding families, and many York Countians held slaves well into the nineteenth century.

From its inception, York County had been a natural thoroughfare for runaway slaves. Many sought the comparative safety found east of the Susquehanna River, Philadelphia being a prime destination. The distant city allowed runaways to assimilate into a larger free black community, find work and, come the 1830s, seek help from the several antislavery offices located in the city.

Freedom seekers' efforts to move eastward predate the bridging of the Susquehanna, which did not occur in either Wrightsville or Harrisburg until around the War of 1812. Such crossings typically required the assistance of friendly locals. As early as 1764, a York County slave named Moses Grimes made multiple attempts to cross the Susquehanna and realize his freedom. Grimes, according to one of his owners, "used to be a hostler, and to wait in a tavern[.]" Even prior to the American Revolution, Grimes's owner feared he would find sympathetic people to assist him: "it is likely he will pass for a free man, and get somebody to forge a pass for him."[162]

Within another twenty years, runaways from the South would find their way to York with increasing regularity. In 1788, the York jail recorded two men from North Carolina and one from Potomac Falls, Virginia. Devoid of sympathy, Michael Graybell, York's jailer, advertised for the "owner or owners of any of the above described negroes" to "come within 4 weeks from the date hereof, otherwise they will be sold for their fees."[163]

Graybell's approach was in line with the prevailing sentiment. Many residents looked on uneasily at the growing population of free blacks. When fifty-six emancipated slaves from Virginia passed through York in 1819, the town's leading papers expressed their displeasure at the "consternation and conjecture" it caused. Much like in Franklin County, locals feared that newly freed slaves would compete for their jobs.

As a result, colonization appealed to many York Countians as the best solution. The American Colonization Society sent traveling lecturers to York, where they solicited memberships for one dollar per person. In 1819, locals organized the York County Colonization Society. The movement attracted the leading citizens of York, who eagerly lent their influence to the society. The York chapter's president, Jacob Barnitz, was a community leader and Revolutionary War veteran. His son-in-law, Samuel Bacon, obtained a federal appointment to oversee former-slave resettlement in Liberia, a colony established on the west coast of Africa. (However, Bacon soon contracted malaria, to which he succumbed in May 1820.)

Not all favored colonization. Like John Peck in Carlisle, Samuel Mars, a free black man from New York, organized local opposition. In 1833, a meeting of York's black citizens declared the American Colonization Society the "greatest foe to the free colored and slave population[.]" African Americans in York drew their opposition to colonization in large part from the works of William Lloyd Garrison (as had Peck). Benjamin Clark, a free black in York, lauded Garrison as "the early, able and consistent friend of the colored population" and urged fellow African Americans and abolitionists to "sustain" the *Liberator*, which he called "the pioneer in the great cause of immediate emancipation."

Black businessman William C. Goodridge, who had been born into slavery in Maryland, actively attended black rights conventions and assisted freedom seekers on the Underground Railroad. Goodridge was the epitome of the man who had everything to lose—a successful businessman, he owned the five-story Centre Hall in downtown York, then the largest building in the entire county. His thriving business sold a variety of medical products and household goods and later included a photographic studio. Risking it all for a cause he believed in, Goodridge used both his Philadelphia Street house and extensive business contacts to help fugitives across the Susquehanna.

His use of rail cars made convenient cover for concealing fugitives, who were often transported by rail to Philadelphia. Just across the river in Columbia, Goodridge likely cooperated with William Whipper and Stephen Smith, free black abolitionists who were involved in the railroad and lumber businesses. Transporting fugitives to and from the rail cars, Goodridge could rely on a wealth of black support. One estimate indicates that nearly half the adult black male population of South Central Pennsylvania was involved in refugees' aid societies by the 1840s.[164]

White abolitionists also had a lengthy legacy in York. A notable Quaker presence helped to ferment antislavery beliefs. Abolitionists also came from out of state, such as Jonathan Jessop, a North Carolina native who had moved to York with his widowed mother at age thirteen. By the time he reached adulthood, Jessop was employing free blacks at his farm. Freedom seekers reaching York would be concealed by Jessop's workers under hay in his barn. His grandson Edward J. Chalfant, born in 1836, came of age distributing "anti-slavery documents and papers" throughout York.[165]

ELSEWHERE, LOCALS BRAVED PUBLIC sentiment to articulate their antislavery beliefs. In northern York County, abolitionist Eli Lewis founded Lewisberry in 1798. The entire Lewis family was heavily engaged in the reform movements of the day, ranging from temperance and education to abolition. One of his sons, Dr. Webster Lewis, was integral in organizing an Underground Railroad network through the northern half of the county. He was "in constant communication with…Joel Wierman and William Wright of Adams County." His son, Dr. Robert Nebinger Lewis, continued to advocate abolition, even after a slave catcher attempted to shoot him. Lewis cheated death when the pistol misfired at the critical moment.[166]

Along the banks of the Susquehanna, in Wrightsville, descendants of the town's founders were steady friends to the fugitive. In the late eighteenth century, Susannah Wright married Jonathan Mifflin, and the couple lived in a well-situated house overlooking the river. Their son Samuel Wright Mifflin carried on their tradition as they grew older. Well into the 1840s, the family's "trusty boatman," Robert Loney, paddled fugitives across the river at night.

Children such as Samuel Mifflin were raised to view such activities as an extension of their faith. That their lives were often disrupted or endangered in giving aid to complete strangers meant little in the grander scheme of things. Interruptions in their daily routines were sporadic and could happen at any time. One day, Samuel Mifflin came home to find thirteen fugitive slaves in the family parlor. They had been found "wandering in the neighborhood" by his older brother, who quickly brought them home. "The windows were closed to prevent discovery, and a lamp kept burning during the day," noted one account. Two nights of bad weather prevented a crossing until, on the third evening, they were conveyed across the Susquehanna by Loney.[167]

Although not as tightly organized as their neighbors in Adams County, York County's diverse lot of abolitionists were extremely active, both publicly and covertly. Men like Robert Nebinger Lewis needed little reminder of the inherent danger of their work, but a court case in nearby Carlisle would soon reveal that even sympathy with local blacks was enough to put one's life—and liberty—in jeopardy.

CHAPTER 6

"THIS IS THE LANGUAGE OF AMERICA"

COLUMBIA, DAUPHIN AND EASTWARD

East of the Susquehanna River, abolitionists were able to operate with comparatively more freedom. Large free black populations in Harrisburg and Columbia provided strong bases of support and gave abolitionists added security to speak their minds—or break the law to aid freedom seekers.

Columbia's black population skyrocketed in 1819, when 56 manumitted slaves of a Virginia planter settled there (the same 56 freed slaves who had caused "consternation and conjecture" while passing through York). With assistance from local Quakers, they settled in the northeastern part of Columbia. They were joined in 1821 by nearly 100 more freed slaves, manumitted by a Virginia Quaker. The addition of the Wrightsville bridge a decade earlier made Columbia a hub for runaway slaves and abolitionists alike. By 1830, 20 percent of Columbia's 2,046 residents were black.

Stephen Smith was born a term slave in Paxtang township, Dauphin County. He was manumitted before the age of twenty-eight and offered work in a Columbia lumberyard. However, when Smith was around ten years old, he had witnessed an attempted kidnapping of his mother, who remained a slave. The incident left a lasting impact on him. Smith worked extra hours, saving money, buying small amounts of lumber and reselling it at a profit. His wife also contributed, running an oyster and refreshment house to garner additional funds. By the 1830s, Smith had amassed a large and profitable business and was one of Columbia's wealthiest citizens, white or black.

His rapid success, against the backdrop of the town's budding black population, soon incited jealousy. In August 1834, race riots broke out. Windows of black homes were shattered, and in some parts, mob violence ensued. Many black residents fled their town, fearing for their lives. On September 2, 1834, another mob ransacked Smith's Front Street office, making it clear that successful black men were not welcome. Afterward, Smith advertised "my entire stock of lumber, either wholesale or retail, at a reduced price, as I am determined to close my business at Columbia." He would finally leave Columbia in 1842 and settle in Philadelphia. His lumber business, however, remained closely intertwined with the actual railroad as well as the Underground one. In coordination with York's William Goodridge, rail cars owned by Smith were used to transport freedom seekers from Wrightsville and Columbia to Philadelphia.[168]

When it came to mob violence, the response from local authorities was less than sympathetic. A committee of Columbia's leading white citizens argued that "the Colonization Society ought to be supported by all the citizens favorable to the removal of the blacks from the country." They also deemed "the preachers of immediate abolition and amalgamation to be considered as political incendiaries, and regarded with indignation and abhorrence."[169]

Even some local abolitionists agreed with the last sentiment and sought to prevent public abolition lecturing. William and Deborah Wright, Quakers living in Columbia, were close allies of Smith. Together, the couple operated an important Underground Railroad station. Fugitives from Adams County oftentimes made their way through stations near Gettysburg, through York County, and with aid from William Goodridge, crossed the Wrightsville covered bridge into Columbia. Generally, Goodridge's black carriage driver, Cato Jourdon, "brought all 'baggage' safely across" the bridge.[170] However, as Friends, the Wrights preferred to follow the tradition of Quaker modesty. Deborah Wright regarded roving abolitionist lecturers and their confrontational style as doing more harm than good. In August 1835, a year after the Columbia race riots, Wright told abolitionist lecturers "that this was not the place for them to Lecture in[.]" She hoped that "every care may be taken here, to avoid excitement."

She also differed from abolitionists in Adams County, who had for years defended the right of "free speech" when publishing provocative antislavery tracts. Deborah Wright called these "obnoxious papers," which would only arouse the "fever of apprehension of general bloodshed" in the southern states and foil "minds that may be seeking—silently seeking means to do away with the National sin." In another letter, she related her difficulty defending the antislavery cause while in discussion with a Presbyterian friend, who noted that most lecturers were in the pay of antislavery societies in New York or London—so-called hirelings, whom some Quakers argued were reliant on money, flattered with worldly power and contradicted Quaker ideals of plainness.[171]

Despite their nonconfrontational style, the Wrights remained involved in secretive Underground Railroad activity. "[A]t this moment there is a colored man waiting for thy uncles advice," Deborah wrote to a nephew in 1835. "I, have given direction of his breakfast and it is probable he will tarry till sunup—but we really are at a loss to know where to direct him."[172]

In Harrisburg, the presence of statewide antislavery conventions helped to encourage a "tolerance, if not acceptance," of abolitionist presence. There, a budding black community, concentrated around the capitol grounds, played host to leading abolitionists. Abby Kelley, who had also lectured in Adams County, spoke in Harrisburg to considerable fanfare (not all positive, however). In 1839, Charles B. Ray, one of the editors of the *Colored American* newspaper, visited the city to push his serial. Ray was encouraged by what he termed the "respectable" and "industrious" nature of Harrisburg's black community but found them "too timid, too much afraid of the storm."

Ray's comments may have been overly harsh. Harrisburg's black community had organized the African Methodist Episcopal Society in 1817, and Minister Jacob D. Richardson had helped spearhead opposition to local colonization sentiment. "[W]e hold these truths to be self-evident," read a resolution crafted by Harrisburg blacks in 1819, "that all men (black and white, poor and rich) are born free and equal; that they are endowed by their Creator with life, liberty and the pursuit of happiness. This is the language of America, of reason, and of eternal truth."[173]

In Harrisburg, black faith leaders were often intertwined in the work of the Underground Railroad. Edward Bennett, a chimney sweep and deacon in the church, was among those involved. By the late 1820s, he and his wife, Mary Ann, were the city's leading "conductors," likely working with William Rutherford, a white man who owned a farm just east of town.[174]

Harrisburg's African American community also had a lengthy history of resisting attempts to recapture fugitive slaves. In April 1825, a Maryland slaveholder had sought to return south with a recaptured runaway, only to be confronted by a "great number of blacks" who were reportedly "armed with clubs and cudgels." As the Marylander descended the courthouse steps, they "rushed furiously upon him, and attempted a rescue." A "squabble" ensued, and "one of the Marylanders fired a pistol, after having received several blows from the assailants, and wounded one of the blacks in the arm." The slave owner and his allies rushed off to a nearby hotel but apparently still feared for their lives, as the same group of African Americans "gathered about the door, and after some time another fracas took place." Local authorities finally intervened, and nineteen African Americans were arrested, twelve of whom were later found guilty and sentenced to jail time.[175] Despite their defeat, they had made it clear that slave catchers would not go about their business uncontested in Harrisburg.

By the 1850s, William M. Jones, an African American "doctor" or healer around sixty years of age, had emerged as a leader in Harrisburg's black community. Jones owned a boardinghouse that was widely suspected as a shelter for runaway slaves. When the new Fugitive Slave Law of 1850 brought the appointment of Harrisburg's own U.S. commissioner to return runaways, the unabashedly proslavery Richard McAllister, Jones helped organize the resistance. He alerted abolitionist lawyers to the plight of fugitives who had come to the city, offered (often dubious) testimony to protect accused runaways and even participated in more courthouse "squabbles" as a last resort to free captured fugitives.[176]

To the southeast, in Middletown, an African American community centered around Five Points—a distinctive set of five gable-pointed town houses on the southwestern corner of Catherine and Main Streets—was laden with abolitionist sentiment. Various black families were leading actors on the Underground Railroad route that ran through Middletown and specifically Five Points. Mary Brown, a resident of Five Points, hailed from Virginia and was likely a former slave. She was widely regarded as a female conductor on the Underground, as were members of the Crow and Fisher families. While not all actively participated in the Underground Railroad, many had experienced it firsthand. The Gordon family had escaped from slavery in Staunton, Virginia, opting to settle in Middletown. East of the Susquehanna, they found a level of safety and freedom unknown to them in bondage or even in the counties west of the river.[177]

CHAPTER 7

"THE ATMOSPHERE WAS CHARGED"

COLLEGES AND THE ABOLITION QUESTION

At Dickinson College in Carlisle, slavery had been debated by northern and southern students since the 1780s. Founded by abolitionist Benjamin Rush in 1783, the school grew rapidly. By the 1830s, the college had garnered a reputation throughout the Mid-Atlantic, drawing nearly half its students from Maryland and Virginia alone.[178] Although many of the faculty—including the college's president, Robert Emory—held antislavery views, they generally restricted these to private conversations or personal correspondence, taking care not to cause disturbances among the student body, at risk of jeopardizing half of the college's incoming tuition fees.

In Carlisle, however, the question of slavery was increasingly hard to avoid. In 1844, Cumberland County had been heavily canvassed by both Whigs and Democrats, the annexation of Texas (and addition of more slave territory) being the primary issue of the campaign. The Whigs, who nominated Henry Clay, went down to defeat both in Cumberland County and nationally to Democratic nominee James Polk, who carried the day in favor of annexation. Shortly into Polk's term, the Mexican War began, and as American victory looked more certain, a new national debate raged over the future of slavery in what would become New Mexico, Arizona, California, Nevada and Utah.

As if that were not enough, fugitive slave ads were routinely placed alongside notices for horses, cows and other advertisements in Carlisle's papers. A few miles to the south, in Boiling Springs, Daniel Kaufman,

Dickinson College, circa 1861. *Library of Congress.*

a longtime Underground Railroad operative, had just been busted for sheltering thirteen freedom seekers in his barn. With a plethora of witnesses from his own town willing to testify against him, by 1847, Kaufman was under trial at the county courthouse in Carlisle, his legal counsel none other than Thaddeus Stevens. (Despite the fanfare, he would ultimately be convicted at a second trial in Federal court in 1852 and fined $4,191.)[179]

It was that same county courthouse that Professor John McClintock of Dickinson College strolled by nearly every day on his way to the post office. Born in Philadelphia in 1814, McClintock was a studious academic, an upstanding Methodist scholar who also had a vitriolic hatred of slavery. He was an avid reader of newspapers and closely followed political events concerning slavery. "I shall strain every nerve to rebuke this abominable Texas inquiry with pen and tongue," he had written in the midst of the 1844 presidential contest. "The days of the Republic are numbered, and of right ought to be, if by its means slavery is extended one inch, or prolonged in its wretched existence one hour."[180] In another letter, he confided, "I feel it in my bones that I shall devote a good part of my life to this great evil."[181] They were feelings that did not waver or taper off. "To tell the truth," he wrote in December 1846, "my abhorrence of slavery grows apace. Year after year I feel more and more that something should be done by every good man in this land to deliver it."[182]

ON WEDNESDAY, JUNE 2, 1847, the thirty-two-year-old McClintock happened to be crossing the square when postmaster George Sanderson hollered to him from the courthouse steps: "Don't you want to see that case?" McClintock, oblivious to the day's happenings, replied, "What?" "A habeas corpus of three fugitives," was Sanderson's retort.

"This was the first knowledge I had of the case," McClintock later penned, "and I went into the Court Room." Shuffling through the crowded chamber, he took a seat alongside the counsel representing three fugitive slaves. From his vantage point "near the bench," McClintock's keen eye quickly began to piece together the situation.[183] The aggrieved parties, or those whom the law recognized as such, were two brothers-in-law from Hagerstown, Maryland, by the names of Howard Hollingsworth and James Kennedy. The duo had been hot on the trail of their escaped slaves, recapturing them near Shippensburg. Intent on following the law to the letter, lest any nuances in the Pennsylvania legal code would set their slaves free, Kennedy and Hollingsworth took their human property to the county courthouse, where they sought formal permission to return to Maryland with their slaves.[184]

Their fears were not unfounded. Dating back to the early days of George Washington's administration, northern state governments (especially that of Pennsylvania) had proven reluctant to return fugitive slaves south. In 1791, Pennsylvania governor Thomas Mifflin had sought to extradite three Virginia citizens accused of kidnapping a black man, named John Davis, when his owner had failed to comply with the terms of Pennsylvania's Gradual Abolition law. A lengthy correspondence between the respective governors ensued, in which the Virginia governor accused Pennsylvanians of "seducing and harboring the slaves of the Virginians." Ultimately, the dispute prompted President Washington to push for the Fugitive Slave Law of 1793, which empowered southerners to seize escaped slaves and return south with them.[185]

In 1826, Pennsylvania enacted a protective law that required slave owners or their agents to appear before a local judge before returning home with those they claimed as fugitive slaves. Under this new law, the burden of proof now rested upon the slaveholder, who was required to provide a legal affidavit from his home county or township, containing a physical description of the escaped slave. Upon review, a local judge would decide whether the alleged fugitive standing before him matched the physical description.[186] Nevertheless, this law was oftentimes ignored, especially in isolated areas where free blacks or runaway slaves did not have a community that would notice their absence and stand up for them.

This was not true of Carlisle, which for years had had a highly active Underground Railroad operation, mostly run by African Americans. The black barber John Peck, until leaving Carlisle in the early 1840s, had been the unofficial leader of the cell.[187] The slaves in the courtroom on June 2 had many connections to Carlisle. James Kennedy claimed ownership of Hester, a woman who was married to George Norman, a free man living in Carlisle. The other two slaves, whom the Hollingsworth family sought to recapture, were a man named Lloyd Brown and his ten-year-old daughter, Ann.

When the session had convened earlier that morning, the presiding judge was satisfied with the evidence Kennedy and Hollingsworth had presented. They were given a certificate officially delivering the slaves into their custody, but the slaves would be kept in the Carlisle jail until the owners were ready to make their return. Satisfied, the slaveholders prepared to leave the room when Norman made a herculean effort to rescue his wife from the hands of the sheriff's assistant, Robert McCartney. Acting alone, however, Norman was quickly subdued by McCartney, and Hester, along with Hollingsworth's slaves, was taken back to the jail.

Meanwhile, a Whig lawyer obtained a writ of habeas corpus, and a hearing was scheduled for four o'clock that afternoon. While McClintock remained blissfully unaware, ensconced on campus or in his West Louther Street home, a number of black residents gathered outside the courthouse. Judge Samuel Hepburn convened the court at four, as McClintock was just beginning to make his way toward the square. Judge Hepburn brought Kennedy and Hollingsworth up on a warrant for forcibly entering the home where they had found the escaped slaves. As the two slaveholders wrangled up bail money, a group of blacks attempted to rush the prisoners' box and free Hester, but McCartney drew his pistol and aimed menacingly at the front line of the crowd, thwarting yet another attempt to rescue Norman's wife.

Professor John McClintock as he would have appeared in 1847. *Archives and Special Collections, Dickinson College.*

Only then did McClintock, beckoned by Sanderson, finally arrive. The proceedings "nearly over," he listened as Judge Hepburn ruled that, despite the new developments, the certificate issued that morning was still valid. The men could return, slaves in tow, to Hagerstown. Spurred to action, McClintock spoke with Hepburn, "asking him the precise state of the case; and whether the new law of 1846–7 was in force." This law, one of a wave of new antislavery protective acts put in place throughout the North in the 1840s, prohibited any state officer to assist in the return of fugitive slaves. Cumberland County's judiciary and law enforcement had violated this new law, only passed on March 3, 1847, by holding the fugitives in the county prison while Kennedy and Hollingsworth made preparations for their return home.

To McClintock's shock, Hepburn replied that he "had not seen it, & asked if I was sure that it had passed." The professor was sure, and when asked if he had a "certified copy," McClintock replied no, but he did have a copy of the newspaper in which the law was printed. Obligingly, he would return home and retrieve it for Hepburn's convenience.

"About this time," remembered McClintock, "there was a melee in the court-room, the nature of which I did not understand. I passed down to the door of the court-room & saw a coloured man near the door, whom I had known as a decent man, apparently in danger. A man (Foulke) had a mace or long stick in his hand raised threateningly to the best of my recollection—he said to the Negro, 'You ought to have your brains knocked out' or 'your scull broke.'" The black man, possibly George Norman, told both the man named Foulke and McClintock that "he had done nothing," to which McClintock replied that "if he was struck or injured, to apply to me & I would see that justice was done him."

McClintock walked home, retrieved the newspaper and delivered it to the attorney representing the fugitives. Thinking this was the conclusion of an already exciting day, McClintock and some others walked out to the courthouse steps, only to look on as "the coloured people were brought out to be led into the carriage which was drawn out immediately in front of the Courthouse. I anticipated no outbreak, & indeed was sure that the people would be taken off in the carriage." His eyes, however, quickly glanced at a restless, shifting crowd gathered outside the courthouse, largely composed of the town's black population. What happened next, even McClintock claimed not to fully grasp. "Either," he later wrote, "they attempted to escape, or others attempted to rescue them; blows were struck, as far as I could judge, by the white men first, & a general riot with missiles ensued."[188]

The "fray," wrote the *Hagerstown News*, "was of a very general character; the whites, upon seeing the disregard of the negroes for the decision of the court, and their bold attempt to trample upon the laws of the State, generally rallied in aid of the owners of the slaves." The proslavery paper indicated that "[n]umbers of students of Dickinson College, who were from the South, also took an active part." Judge Hepburn and the sheriff were at the scene, "busy in securing the arrest of the most prominent negroes rioters. Many of the negroes were severely wounded, and we are told, that at every post and corner was some one to be seen, bloody and bleeding, leaning for support." Pro-southern accounts also fingered "Professor McClintock, of Dickinson College," who they claimed "was particularly conspicuous in urging the negroes to the attack."[189]

James Kennedy was sprinting after his fleeing slaves when he tripped, stumbled to the ground and was trampled by the rush of the mob. After briefly inquiring about Kennedy's health, McClintock made his way home. However, "near the court house corner, I saw two men holding & apparently abusing an old negro woman." Asking the men "if they had authority," McClintock received an indignant response when they pushed the woman to the side. She pleaded her case to the professor, telling him "that she had done nothing, but only attempted to get her old man out of the melee[.]"[190] By publicly intervening on behalf of yet another black citizen, McClintock only further enraged town officials.

"AFTER TEA I HEARD that I was charged with inciting the riot," McClintock recalled, "and that a writ was out against me. All sorts of stories were told, and many of the students were very much excited." The primarily southern student body gathered that evening at the college chapel, where President Robert Emory, a personal friend of McClintock's, tried to soothe injured feelings.[191]

"There was probably not an abolitionist among the students," recalled Moncure Conway, a student and the son of a wealthy slaveholding family in Stafford County, Virginia. "My brother and I, like others, packed our trunks to leave college." Even the respected voice of President Emory could not calm the passions. "[W]e Southerners, wildly excited, appointed a meeting for next morning," wrote Conway. Before they could follow through, McClintock appeared, as "serene" as ever, and "a sudden hush" fell over the room. Calmly, "without any accent of apology or of appeal, he related the simple facts, then descended from the pulpit and moved quickly along the aisle and out of the door." His words gained him the trust of Dickinson's southern students, who soon composed "resolutions of entire confidence" in their professor, signed by all ninety students present.[192] Their resolutions, dispatched to both local and Hagerstown papers, read, in part:

As to Prof. McClintock's alleged participation in the transaction, we are not only satisfied…that the charge is untrue; but from his long established character, we believe him incapable of any such thing. The story, did indeed, come to us at first, so perverted and exaggerated that, with the natural warmth of Southerners, many of us were excited against him. But, after several meetings held for the purpose of considering the matter, in which not only the Southern students, but all the students…participated, we have become convinced of the falsity of the accusation.[193]

The confidence of his students, however, would not protect him from angry locals. Hearing rumors that his house would be mobbed, McClintock brought his family to the relative safety of Emory's home. Potentially in legal jeopardy, McClintock remained pensive, reflecting on the day. "The truth of the case was, that my human and Christian sympathies were openly exhibited on the side of the poor blacks," he wrote, "and this gave mortal offense to the slaveholders and their *confrères* in the town."

The next morning, Emory accompanied McClintock to the town square, where he posted bond for his friend. The trial date was set for August 25, and both sides would have time to prepare their cases. McClintock wanted Thaddeus Stevens to represent him, but it was not compatible with Stevens's current slate of cases. McClintock did not go wanting in support, however, and received an influx of praise from fellow abolitionists. From Philadelphia, James Miller McKim wrote words of encouragement: "Unless Carlisle has greatly changed for the better since I was one of its residents, your liberal views of truth and duty find but little sympathy from those around you….May God strengthen you, and enable you to set your face like a flint….You have a work to do; take counsel only of Him who sends you."[194]

President Emory embarked upon a publicity blitz to protect the college's reputation. "You have no doubt heard of the riot in our town last week," he wrote to a friend in Hagerstown. "Perhaps you have also heard it reported that Prof. McClintock was instigating or encouraging the riot. If you knew him as well as I do, you would know, even without evidence, that that was impossible." Emory also softened McClintock's stance on slavery, adding, "Whatever may be his views on the subject of slavery (& they are by no means so ultra as many imagine) it is contrary to his Principles to attempt to prevent a master's recovering his slaves."[195] Clearly concerned about the response of southern parents, Emory was eager to enclose the "document from Southern Students of the college, [which] will confirm what I wrote to you.…May I beg that you will have it inserted in all the Hagerstown papers that have noticed the affair."[196]

In the meantime, news came that the slaveholder Kennedy had died as a result of his injuries. Even some Carlisle papers castigated McClintock, holding him responsible for the commotion that injured Kennedy. "Emory thinks that I should institute a libel suit against 'The Herald' before the trial comes off here," McClintock wrote on July 1. "All this slander and abuse will work good in the end, not only to the antislavery cause, but to myself personally.…But the parties who have got up the prosecution, backed by the gold of the slaveholders, will strain every nerve to convict me."[197]

When the trial came on August 25, McClintock had as counsel William Morris Meredith, a criminal lawyer and prominent Whig. Several dozen African Americans, accused of involvement in the riot, also stood trial alongside McClintock. During the trial itself, some thirty-six witnesses came forth with strange anecdotes, which prosecutors claimed would prove that McClintock had sinisterly planned the riots. One witness even testified that McClintock's head was "swollen to an unnatural size" on June 2. McClintock's case was well managed, and defense witnesses included a number of fellow Methodists. Some believed the testimony of Jacob Rheem, a prominent citizen and Methodist, may have turned the trial in McClintock's favor. Rheem concurred with much of McClintock's previous account, including that he had urged no one to attack and that whites had "struck the first blows."

The jurors returned a not guilty verdict for McClintock and most of his co-defendants, but the case's most chilling effects came when thirteen African Americans were found guilty. Judge Samuel Hepburn (a Democrat who was less amenable to antislavery views) handed down severe sentences to those found guilty. In an unprecedented move, Hepburn sentenced eleven of the defendants to three years of solitary confinement. McClintock, recognizing a vendetta in the motive, helped to appeal the harsh sentence to the state Supreme Court, where Hepburn's ruling was overturned a year later. The court freed all eleven African Americans, citing time served.

Disgusted at the "heavy course of afflictions…to which I and my family have been subjected," McClintock contemplated leaving Carlisle. "I think of falling back upon the old-fashioned Methodist life," he wrote to Robert Emory. He would leave Carlisle the following year and take up the full-time editorship of the *Methodist Quarterly Review*.[198]

William M. Meredith, the Philadelphia Whig lawyer defending McClintock, was later appointed U.S. secretary of the treasury under President Zachary Taylor. *Library of Congress.*

JOHN MCCLINTOCK WAS NOT the only Pennsylvania professor teaching to a largely southern student body. "It was the fashion of the day for Southern parents to send their boys and girls to Northern institutes or seminaries," recalled Randolph Shotwell, a young Virginian, "chiefly because the expense was a great deal heavier, and the thing sounded better in talking to their neighbors. Besides," he admitted, "the 'imprint'…of the best Southern Schools could never compare with even a second-rate Yankee institution." South Central Pennsylvania—a border region with no shortage of schools— soon became home to a growing number of southern students.

Raised in a slave society, most southern students took exception to local abolitionists, as well as college presidents, administrators and professors who professed antislavery leanings. When Jonathan Blanchard toured South Central Pennsylvania in 1837, he was taunted by southern students at Pennsylvania College in Gettysburg and at Marshall College in Mercersburg (later Franklin & Marshall College). At Marshall, Blanchard claimed to have been threatened "with brute force" by southern students armed with "concealed weapons."[199]

For southern students at Marshall, Mercersburg prompted much angst and unease, even without Blanchard's presence. The town was home to a "large colored population" that "crowded the back streets," extending to "a village of their own" at the foot of the mountain, called (like the settlement near Stevens's Caledonia Furnace) Little Africa. Much like Jack Hopkins at Pennsylvania College, local blacks also worked as janitors and handymen at the college. Students were familiar with Arnold Brooks, "a tall muscular mulatto, full of talk," who served as chief coachman, conducting students in and out of town. David Johnson, a black janitor, made the students' beds and stocked their rooms with wood for their wood stoves.[200]

Similarly, at Dickinson College, African Americans were employed as janitors and handymen. Black employment occasionally drew ire from local whites, such as one 1842 critic who styled himself "A Friend of Dickinson College and the rites of Man." In an anonymous letter sent to the college's administrators, he demanded to know why "must nearly all the minor work of the installation be given to colored people," grousing that "not even a native negrow [*sic*] of this state is imployed [*sic*] in the college" but instead those "who neather [*sic*] contribute by tax nor influence to publick institutions" and "usurp the rites [*sic*] of the sober industri[ou]s white man[.]"[201] Beyond its racist overtones, the anonymous writer's comments about non-Pennsylvania blacks suggests that many employees had migrated from the South, either as a result of manumission or escaping slavery.

Henry Watts, a janitor at Dickinson College, photographed in 1862. *Library of Congress.*

Some miles to the north, Tuscarora Academy in Juanita County offered young men "an opportunity of preparing for College[.]" Special attention would be paid "to the mind, manners, morals, and comfort" of students "from a distance[.]" Tuscarora's location "in the country" appealed to many southern parents, who no doubt appreciated that there would be "no distractions from quiet study, and none of the temptations to vice and dissipation so common to towns and places of public resort....Our aim is to surround the young, as far as practicable, with the influence and restrictions of a well regulated Christian home," an ad for the academy stated, and "to impart manly and noble motives for action, and earnestness in preparing for the solemn realities of life." Its rural location was desirable for more than just tranquility. In an era when deadly epidemics ravaged cities during the summers, Tuscarora offered "*safe breathing*[.]"[202]

When Randolph Shotwell arrived at Tuscarora from Virginia in 1859, he found himself in "Yankee" country yet among many fellow southerners. He counted "half a dozen from Central Alabama, several from Georgia and Florida, and a number from Maryland and Virginia." This was by no means unusual—an 1853 enrollment list included eighty-four Pennsylvanians and twenty-four New Jerseyans alongside twenty Virginians, nine Marylanders and four Alabamians. "There could be no mistaking the nativity of these Southern youngsters," wrote Shotwell.

> *Tall, dark, long-haired, Byronic-collared;—with immense trunks, (which they paid for having taken to their rooms instead of lugging them up on their own shoulders or begging the aid of a class-mate,) and an air of fretful reserve as if very doubtful if they could put up with such surroundings—they betrayed their sunny birth as much by look and manner, as by speech and tobacco spitting. However, none were more prompt to make themselves at home; and by the end of a week it was seen that they had secured the best rooms, the best seats at the table, the pick desks in school, and were taking the lead among students in most respects—except in study.*[203]

Shotwell's experience demonstrates that even in an idyllic countryside setting, the issue of slavery could not be avoided. At Tuscarora, he and his fellow southerners encountered what they termed "the ignorance of the Northern masses in regard to the South and slavery," grounded in an "absurd notion that nearly all Southerners were wealthy, owning slaves by hundreds, and hereditary acres by thousands, leading lives of aristocratic ease and luxury...varied by occasional indulgence in the manly sport of chasing negroes with blood hounds, or Bowie-knifing somebody in revenge for supposititious slights."

Deep-rooted cultural differences were hard to overcome. The sectional divide "flamed...hot and sputtering between the Northern and Southern students, still in their early teens," Shotwell remembered. Feeling that their

A typical 1850s college dorm room, featuring a wood stove. Students at Mercersburg's Marshall College relied on African American janitors to stock their rooms with wood, among other daily tasks. *Juniata County Historical Society.*

northern classmates entertained false impressions of southern life, his brother Hamilton used his 1850s valedictorian address to ask for "a spirit of large-hearted forbearance and patriotism between all sections of the land, that the Union of our ancestors might be perpetuated."

When school was out of session for several weeks, many southern students remained behind, with insufficient time to make a meaningful trip home. During these sojourns, Shotwell and others at Tuscarora "made frequent trips into the surrounding country, to the mountain towns of Mifflin, Lewiston, Bellefonte, Milroy, etc." For curious southerners, these jaunts also provided "some insight into the operations of the mysterious 'Underground Railroad[.]'" On one particular excursion, Shotwell and some friends eyed a "horse bearing a woman's saddle" partly hidden among the bushes. They stopped, only to discover "a gang of half a dozen negro men, most of them young looking, gathered about a comely young white girl, who was giving them dinner out of a well-filled pillow case. All of the darkies were in their

Right: James John Patterson, a student at Tuscarora and then Dickinson, vividly recalled the tense prewar years at South Central Pennsylvania schools. *Archives and Special Collections, Dickinson College*.

Below: The exterior of Tuscarora Academy, a preparatory school in Juniata County attended by both northern and southern students. Debates over slavery were frequent and fiery. *Juniata County Historical Society*.

shirt-sleeves, and several of them were lolling at full length on the moss-covered rocks directly at the feet of [the] girl, who could not have yet reached twenty years of age!" Shotwell cried, with no lack of indignation at the sight of a white woman consorting with black men.

An hour or so later, Shotwell watched "the party straggle out of the bushes, and descend through the valley; the white girl riding and carrying the 'bundles' of the negroes, one of whom, evidently a favorite, walked by her horse's side and talked with her! It was doubtless a 'train' on the Underground Railroad, piloted by some woodsman's daughter," he sneered.[204]

At Dickinson, the McClintock riots seemed a distant memory as the political campaigns of the 1850s riveted the diverse student body. James John Patterson, who also attended Tuscarora, came to Dickinson in the fall of 1856. That year marked the emergence of the newly formed Republican Party, a northern unit that included former Whigs and disgruntled "free soil" Democrats. They chose John C. Frémont, who opposed the extension of slavery, as the party's first ever presidential nominee. His Democratic opponent, Pennsylvanian (and Dickinson graduate) James Buchanan, argued that new states had a constitutional right to include slavery in their constitutions, if they so desired. Patterson recalled the student body assembling to hold a series of mock elections. So divided were the students that each election ended in a virtual tie, and "there were never more than half a dozen votes difference between the two candidates."

Many students, from North and South, "looked for trouble, [and] wanted it," Patterson reminisced. Most of his classmates were of the "fire eating class," he later mused, "and the atmosphere was charged, though an air of restraint held the students in check," preventing physical violence. Heated discussions were common across campus. Samuel Beck, a classmate from Chestertown, Maryland, "could not be in a group ten minutes without starting an argument" over slavery and national politics, according to Patterson. He remembered only one southern student, a Kentuckian named Duke Slavens, "who could sit down and dispassionately discuss the issues." While others preferred to "stay out of all arguments" and focus on their studies or sleep, few could avoid the ever-present issue.[205]

THE MCCLINTOCK AFFAIR AND new tensions at the college "only accentuated the bitterness that existed in those years," recalled Daniel Kaufman, the Boiling Springs Underground operative. The air of "increased animosity," he wrote, "made more perilous the lot of the agent of the underground railway if detected in his calling." As a result, the primary route of the Underground Railroad through Cumberland County underwent drastic changes. Kaufman, too well known, stepped back, and the route fell to John Morrison and Richard Woods, who lived just southwest of Carlisle, adjacent to each other. From Stevens's Caledonia Furnace in Adams County, freedom seekers were led by Michael Buck, known as a "full blooded African and protege of Woods." Buck routinely traveled in excess of twenty miles from Caledonia to Woods's farm, where runaways were concealed in a thick swamp on the property.[206]

The new connecting link to Harrisburg came in an unexpected form. John Harder, a "market man" and Democrat, was the last person who would be fingered as an Underground Railroad operative. In South Central Pennsylvania, where most abolitionists were as well known for their public advocacy as their widely suspected Underground activity, Harder managed to flip the script. Beyond his political affiliation, Harder's occupation naturally involved transporting goods to market in his "old fashioned Conestoga market wagon." Whenever "passengers" arrived at Richard Woods's farm, a messenger would seek out Harder to inform him. In the meantime, the runaways would be "transferred" from Woods's house a few miles east to Stephen Weakley's farm near Boiling Springs (Weakley was the brother-in-law of Daniel Kaufman). At night, Harder would drive his wagon to Weakley's and load up with "packages" for the "Harrisburg market."[207]

As the 1850s dawned, Harder and his fellow abolitionists would soon see more "packages" than ever before. Attempts to crack down on abolitionists and the work of the Underground Railroad would backfire, resulting in greater public support for abolitionists and those they sought to help.

CHAPTER 8

"SOME HORRIBLE TALES OF CRUELTY"

THE UNDERGROUND RAILROAD IN THE 1850s

A cloudy evening in 1849 found Dr. William Chaplin reclining uneasily in an "elegant carriage," now "woefully travel-stained and mud-bespattered." He had driven along the Baltimore Pike through Westminster and Union Mills, Maryland, and was now within a few miles of Gettysburg. At the front of the carriage, holding the reins, sat a "tall, handsome mulatto," who every few seconds stole an anxious glance backward. Confused, frantic and desperate for his life, he felt almost certain that his brief glimpse of freedom would soon be snatched away from him forever.

Chaplin had been taking fugitives this way in his much-talked-about carriage for several years. Chaplin was the editor of the *National Era*, an abolitionist serial that reported on congressional proceedings, with a special emphasis on slavery subject matter. His well-known antislavery proclivities and frequent presence in the Capitol under the pretense of a journalist enabled the body servants of leading southern congressmen to subtly request his aid.

He had first stumbled upon the three abolitionist families living southeast of Gettysburg in 1846. Chaplin's "quick, keen, restless, gray eyes did not fail to notice the advantages which the hills below the town offered for future contingencies of pursuit," recalled one of the local operatives. The first two farms, situated next to each other, were owned by Cornelius Houghtelin and Adam Wert. Chaplin had gotten familiar with both of these men over the past several years, and he knew they were the link to Gettysburg's most active abolitionist, James McAllister.

A former vice president of the Adams County Anti-Slavery Society, Wert, like his neighbors, had shifted tactics by the late 1840s. Placing less emphasis on vocal opposition to slavery, Wert sought to precipitate slavery's end by aiding runaway slaves in their quest for freedom. His neighbor and friend, James McAllister, was the host of the July 4, 1836 antislavery meeting and also had opted for a more covert solution. By 1849, McAllister's mill, just another mile up the Baltimore Pike, had become the Underground Railroad hub of Gettysburg.

McAllister and each one of his five stout sons—all towering over six feet tall—were extremely active in Underground work. McAllister's property was suited to concealing fugitives. The area surrounding his gristmill was known as Wolf Hill, a craggy, vegetative area remembered by one local as "an almost unexplored wilderness." Locals attributed its name to the presence of wolves on the hill that, even as late as the 1840s (it was rumored), "had not yet been entirely exterminated."

From his seat in the carriage, Dr. Chaplin eyed the Wert farmhouse. He ordered the fugitive driver to bring the two steeds, both foaming at the mouth, to a halt. Leaping "impetuously" down from the carriage, the spry old Chaplin eyed Cornelius Houghtelin and young J. Howard Wert, Adam's nine-year-old son.

"Quick; a guide to the Wolf Hill or this poor man is lost. They are too close behind for me to stay on the turnpike, and I don't know the back route. There they are now," Dr. Chaplin's voice trailed away as the farmer and the farm boy glanced a half mile down the heavily traversed Baltimore Pike, eyeing another team of horses, which "was being urged onward at a frantic speed."

"Jump in, boy, and show him to Jimmy's," Houghtelin shouted. Young Wert catapulted himself into the front of the carriage beside the frightened fugitive. "Drive on: I'll show you," he said. Deviating from the main thoroughfare, they now passed through muddy farm lanes not fit for an "elegant" cosmopolitan carriage of the likes of Chaplin's. Mud caked onto the wheels and

Cornelius Houghtelin as he would have appeared in 1849. Members of the Houghtelin family had been involved in the Adams County Anti-Slavery Society during the 1830s and were known abolitionists. *J. Howard Wert Gettysburg Collection.*

J. Howard Wert, the son of Adam Wert, as a teenager. Wert spent his boyhood and teenage years aiding freedom seekers. *J. Howard Wert Gettysburg Collection.*

then splattered onto the sides of the carriage, the ground damp and moist from an earlier rain. "Better git down to it faster than that, if you want to git away," J. Howard jeered the fugitive. "Fraid to drive down hill, hey?" The levity did little to charm the bewildered fugitive, and soon Wert returned to the pressing work at hand. "Turn up here," he pointed, and the fugitive followed a back lane that was parallel to the Baltimore Pike.

As Wert pointed onward, deeper into the thick woods, the fugitive, "with a dubious look" in his eye, hesitated. His freedom, and very possibly his life, was in imminent danger. Should he trust a nine-year-old boy's driving instructions? At the time, he had no other option. He set off toward the trees where Wert had pointed but was seized with terror when a "triumphant shout" came from behind, where the carriage of his pursuers was less than two hundred yards away.

Grabbing the reins, Wert led the team down a hazardous dirt farm lane, bringing the coach to a halt beneath a towering ledge of ancient granite rocks on Wolf Hill. "We'll stop here," he told the fugitive, leaving him ensconced beneath the rock ledge while he sought out one of the McAllisters. He found young "Aleck" McAllister, one of James McAllister's five "stalwart and daring" sons. Within half an hour, Aleck had managed to hide the fugitive "in a snug rock cave at a point from which, through little apertures in a dense thicket of scrubby pine bushes, there was a glimpse, at a distance of a few yards, of the only roadway that traversed…this wild section."

The fugitive safely hidden, Aleck and Wert returned to find "the worst wrecked carriage that had been seen for many a day." The slave hunters, lacking the local knowledge and the brazen driving skills of nine-year-old Wert, had been unable to make good with their pursuit and eventually abandoned their carriage to continue forward on foot. For several hours, they searched the dense thickets of Wolf Hill, in one instance coming so close to the cave where the fugitive was concealed that, from within, he could make out "their shadowy forms as they passed along the road so near that he could have tossed a stone amongst them." Eventually, the pursuers gave up. Dr. Chaplin, with the assistance of Gettysburg's three leading abolitionist families, had helped a slave "steal" himself.[208]

FOR ABOLITIONISTS EVERYWHERE, MUCH had changed since the movement's early days in the 1830s. Texas had been annexed. Florida had been admitted. The Mexican War had brought new territory into the Union. The question of whether these lands would be "free soil" or slave states soon reignited the debate from thirty years earlier, during the Missouri Crisis.

After considerable wrangling in Congress, President Millard Fillmore signed a package of five compromise bills into law, known as the Compromise of 1850. Pitched as a means to preserve the Union, one of the bills—the Fugitive Slave Law—was regarded with particular disgust among abolitionists. A strengthening of the 1793 law passed during George Washington's administration, the new act was intended to it easier for southern slaveholders to recapture their fugitive slaves. Under the new version, U.S. commissioners—officials who were appointed, not elected—would have the sole authority to decide the fate of runaways. Alleged fugitives were not even allowed to testify in their own defense, and commissioners received ten dollars for each fugitive they returned to slavery, compared to just five dollars if they ruled in favor of freedom. The 1850 act also took precedence over a slew of antislavery measures enacted by northern state legislatures during the past fifty years, including Pennsylvania's 1826 protective act.

Many northerners were infuriated by what had transpired in Washington. The Fugitive Slave Law, J. Howard Wert later wrote, "contained some odious features which aroused a popular feeling of antipathy against slavery itself—an opposition from a large element that had, hitherto, been dormant in the strife." Provisions within the law—especially the pay scale for commissioners—were, in Wert's view, "so palpable a bait to the worst side of an avaricious man that it outraged the people's innate idea of fair play." Negative views of the law "gave an impetus to the U.G.R.R. which the preaching of abolition emissaries had never been able to impart."[209]

Most significantly, the law's intended effect—to intimidate would-be Underground "conductors" with threats of large fines and jail time if caught—actually had the opposite effect. The McAllisters, Werts and other Underground operatives were only emboldened to continue their work. With public sentiment shifting rapidly in their favor, they had increasing

President Millard Fillmore (1850–53) hoped to forge a compromise between northern and southern interests to preserve the Union. The Fugitive Slave Law of 1850 backfired, however, and resulted in wider support of Underground Railroad activities in the North. *Library of Congress.*

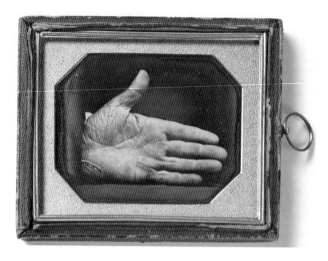

Abolitionists took advantage of new forms of communication, such as photography. With images such as the "Branded Hand"—depicting an abolitionist convicted of "slave stealing" whose palm was branded with the letters "SS"—they hoped to convey the barbarity of the slave system. *Massachusetts Historical Society.*

local support to defend their actions. Across the free states, as far west as Ohio, Indiana, Illinois and Michigan, Underground conductors would find the business of the Underground Railroad arriving at its peak.

Theodore McAllister, one of James McAllister's five sons, later told an interviewer that "1850 to 1858 was the period in which [fugitives] came most frequently." Using typical caution, like many families where clandestine work on the Underground was a way of life, the McAllisters took pain not to speak of the fugitives they helped, even to one another. Any offhand remark concerning the identity or master of a fugitive, if repeated in the wrong setting, could lead to a runaway's recapture. Or a similar slip-up might lead to charges brought against them by a proslavery agent. Already publicly identified as members of a local antislavery society, they were widely suspected of Underground work and had to remain constantly vigilant to protect both the fugitives and themselves. Families such as the McAllisters understood that the less they knew and spoke about the individuals they helped, the safer they all were.

Theodore, who was eight when the Fugitive Slave Law was passed, recalled that "many of these fugitives were neither seen nor heard of by any other member of our large family except myself until they were far on their way to Canada. But there were never any questions asked if quantities of rations disappeared from [the] cellar and pantry." He also found old clothing placed "very convenient to my hand" in the attic. He and the other McAllister boys usually hid fugitives "under the lower floor and in the cog pit" of the mill or among the various caves and hiding spots on Wolf Hill, such as Aleck had done for the man Dr. Chaplin had brought in 1849.

Fascinated by the constant influx of strangers, young Theodore spent many a night "crouched" in the small hiding spaces in the mill, listening "to some horrible tales of cruelty told by those young—mostly yellow men, some of them with features of the white race, as they rested their weary legs and filled themselves up in preparation for another race." Most of the runaways he spoke to declared, without hesitation, that they would never return "alive to see mothers, wives, sisters torn from their families, lashed together and driven off like cattle to some far Southern slave mart."[210]

In northern Adams County, near York Springs, Joel Wierman and his wife, Lydia Lundy, joined in defying the new law. Her brother Benjamin Lundy had died in 1839, but she and her husband continued to carry out his legacy. Along with neighbors and in-laws William and Phebe Wright, they had been active participants in the Underground Railroad for decades. In 1851, shortly after the law's passage, the Wiermans witnessed the heartbreaking moment when a fugitive slave, concealed in their barn but "tiring of the monotony," went out "into the corn field where there were some men at work."

The slave owner and his party soon appeared, "fresh from their search at William Wright's," and eyed the fugitive. A desperate chase ensued, and the runaway dove into a stream, emerging to hear shouts "that if he persisted, they would shoot him, they having fair aim." He froze and was soon recaptured. Both abolitionist families watched in horror as "[h]is hands were tied behind him, the master holding the rope[.]" Phebe Wright "quoted Scripture to the master, and used every argument she was mistress of, to induce him to promise not to sell Sam to the far South." Their efforts were in vain.[211]

Although heartbreaking, this case was the exception rather than the norm. During the 1850s, the vast majority of runaway slaves made their way successfully to freedom. "After their arrival in this place, the fugitives become invisible," declared one Harrisburg editor. "Nobody 'knows nothing' about their whereabouts." Local papers churned out reports of escapes, often with a tone of bemusement. "The Underground Railroad continues to do a large business," reported a Harrisburg newspaper. "A colored individual, who seems to be thoroughly 'booked up,' informs us that, within two months, not less than eighteen slaves have passed through Harrisburg[.]" Many would have agreed with the editor of Harrisburg's *Morning Herald*, when he declared the Fugitive Slave Law "a dead letter."[212]

President Franklin Pierce (1853–57) was a deeply controversial figure. His signing of the Kansas-Nebraska Act in May 1854 reignited the national conflict over slavery. *Library of Congress.*

As the Underground ramped up, Washington reached a new crisis. Eager for a final solution to the slavery problem, Illinois senator Stephen Douglas proposed the Kansas-Nebraska Act. Advocating "popular sovereignty," the act would discard the Missouri Compromise's geographic line between free and slave states and allow territories to hold popular referendums on whether to legalize slavery within their borders. President Franklin Pierce, a Democrat from New Hampshire, signed the bill into law, amid outcries from abolitionists.

Abolitionists viewed "popular sovereignty" as a sinister power grab by slaveholders. "More, more, your cry is still for more," wrote a Vermont pamphleteer. "You must have States, you must have votes in the Senate[.]"[213] Rhode Island abolitionist Francis Wayland encouraged his audiences to "consider this as a bill to establish slavery throughout all this vast region."[214] From afar, Englishman Edward Baines declared the Kansas-Nebraska bill "one of the greatest calamities that could have befallen mankind" because it allowed "an indefinite extension of the system of Slavery."[215]

The calamity would also prove the undoing of Pierce's presidency. As soon as the bill was signed, a flood of proslavery and free-state settlers rushed into the Kansas territory, intent on winning the popular referendum on slavery. When the votes were finally counted, proslavery settlers came out on top, but the contest was far from over. Free staters alleged that violence, voter intimidation and corruption had been used in securing the victory. In protest, free-staters met in Topeka, drawing up the "Topeka Constitution," which formed a government based on antislavery principles. Proslavery settlers denied its legitimacy and, in response, drafted their own "Lecompton Constitution." With two rival governments both claiming to represent the people of Kansas, both sides resorted to armed violence as they sought to gain the upper hand.

CHAPTER 9

"IT...WOULD ARRAY THE WHOLE COUNTRY AGAINST US"

JOHN BROWN'S RAID, 1859

One man particularly enraged by the Kanas debacle was John Brown. Born in Connecticut in 1800, Brown had been something of a wandering abolitionist, claiming residency in numerous states. He was raised a Calvinist, and his religious hatred of slavery ran deep. What set him apart from other abolitionists was his belief that slavery could not be ended peacefully.

To his sons, he emphasized his "determination to make war on slavery" and had them each swear an oath of "secresy [*sic*] and devotion to the purpose of fighting slavery by force of arms to the extent of our ability."[216] The situation in Kansas, then, fit Brown's definition of abolitionism perfectly.

Brown went to Kansas looking for a fight. In "Bleeding Kansas," conflicts were not hard to find. For months, proslavery Missourians had crossed the border and murdered many leading free-staters, who retaliated in kind. Infuriated, Brown felt it his duty to respond to southern aggression. "Something is going to be done now," he told his family in May 1856. "We must show by actual work that there are two sides to this thing and that they cannot go on with impunity." Soon after arriving, Brown drew up a plan to attack proslavery leaders in their homes along Kansas's Pottawatomie Creek.

What followed became known as the "Pottawatomie Massacre." In the middle of the night, Brown and his followers entered the cabins of proslavery settlers, led them out at gunpoint and savagely murdered them with sword thrusts and gunshots. Brown chose five victims in all, justifying his actions by citing the men's proslavery proclivities.

John Brown is photographed by Augustus Washington, an African American photographer in Hartford, Connecticut, circa 1846–47. Raising his right hand as if swearing an oath against slavery, with his left Brown holds the flag of the Subterranean Pass-Way, his militarized version of the Underground Railroad. *National Portrait Gallery, Smithsonian Institution.*

After the outrage of his initial foray, Brown fought again in August 1856. There, he engaged three hundred proslavery Missourians near the town of Osawatomie. Although Brown's men retreated after inflicting minimal casualties, the symbolism of the fight was not lost on many northerners. His son John Jr. glowingly praised his father's actions: "This has proved most unmistakably that 'Yankees' WILL 'fight.'"[217]

When he left Kansas, Brown emerged an extremely controversial figure. Hated by southerners, he enjoyed mixed popularity among northern audiences. While some abolitionists praised his willingness to fight, others recoiled at his violent methods. Embracing his image as the fighting abolitionist, Brown toured the Northeast, visiting prominent abolitionists in hopes of securing their financial support for his new plan—to open a corridor along the Appalachian Mountain range and encourage slaves to flee northward.

At the New York home of black abolitionist Frederick Douglass, Brown drafted a constitution to govern the territory he planned to capture.[218] Over time, however, Brown's vision morphed from what he originally presented to Douglass. By 1859, his plan would include an armed assault on the federal armory at Harpers Ferry, Virginia, and distributing weapons to local enslaved populations.

IN THE SUMMER OF 1859, Brown chose Chambersburg, Pennsylvania, as one of two staging areas for his planned attack. Not only was it conveniently located up the valley from Harpers Ferry, Virginia, but an existing Underground Railroad structure could also support him. Henry Watson, the black barber who figured prominently in Chambersburg's Underground cell, assisted Brown.

Once he had made contact with Watson, Brown moved on to southern Maryland, where he established a second staging area in a farmhouse near Sharpsburg, Maryland. Over the next several months, Brown familiarized himself with the surrounding country, making frequent trips from Chambersburg to Harpers Ferry and back again. Brown and his compatriots took lodging in Mary Ritner's boardinghouse on East King Street, where he identified himself as Isaac Smith and listed his occupation as a mine speculator. It was likely no coincidence Brown chose Mary Ritner's boardinghouse. Her father-in-law was former Pennsylvania governor Joseph Ritner, who, in the late 1830s, had earned a reputation as an antislavery politician. In all likelihood, Mary Ritner was aware of Brown's true identity, if not his exact plans. She must have known something was up when "Isaac Smith" required "three guards at different doors" when interviewing a local candidate for hauling "hardware" to Harpers Ferry.

The Mary Ritner boardinghouse, 225 East King Street, Chambersburg. John Brown and his men boarded here while planning their assault on Harpers Ferry. *Franklin County Historical Society.*

Under his assumed name, Brown made a good impression on most locals he encountered. Ritner's young daughter Emma Jane recalled him as a "strong and vigorous" man, universally adored by the local children. "He stayed only a few days but all through the summer he came at intervals. The understanding was that they had bought a farm and were buying farming tools....My sister and I often rode with him for a mile or two and walked back," she wrote.

Emma was struck by Brown's "manliness" and Christian beliefs, which were on display when she brought home a lost African American child. Her mother and John Brown were seated in the dining room as she entered, pulling the child by the hand. "The effect on Brown was electrical," recalled Franklin Keagy, a fellow boarder. "He took both the children in his arms. His enthusiasm knew no bounds. His eyes sparked. His face became radiant as if his heart and mind had received new inspiration." He declared Emma's charitable act "the grandest act he ever beheld, and a sight worthy of the Angels[.]"

However, Emma was unaware of what lay concealed in Brown's "white canvas covered wagon." As he played the part of the homely, soft-spoken old man, Brown was gathering weapons and supplies for his intended raid. Henry Watson acted as a "general agent to forward men, mail and freight." Watson and his wife, Eliza, housed black members of Brown's small "army." The barber would also prove a critical connection when Brown sought the endorsement of the country's leading black abolitionist, Frederick Douglass.

Frederick Douglass as he appeared in January 1862. By the 1850s, the graying Douglass was the most famous African American in the country. *Library of Congress.*

"About three weeks before the raid on Harper's Ferry, John Brown wrote to me," Douglass later explained. Brown felt Douglass's support would lend "the venture the air of credibility" and rally free blacks to his side. However, Douglass's notoriety complicated things, and he was instantly recognized upon arrival in Chambersburg in mid-August. Urged to speak, Douglass lectured at the town hall to a mixed reception. Anti-black sentiment remained strong in Franklin County, and the editors of the *Franklin Repository* lashed out at "this woolly headed son of Africa, Fred. Douglas," who was "dropped so suddenly and unexpectedly into our midst."[219]

The day before, Douglass had "called upon Mr. Henry Watson, a simple-minded and warm-hearted man, to whom Capt. Brown had imparted the secret of my visit, to show me the road to the appointed rendezvous." As Brown was both a well-known and wanted man (still at large for the murders at Pottawatomie Creek), his cover could not be compromised. "Watson was very busy in his barber's shop," Douglass wrote, "but he dropped all and put me on the right track."

Douglass and Watson approached "the old quarry" outside town—the location designated for their meeting—with caution. They knew Brown's trigger-happy reputation and feared startling the "old man." Douglass soon eyed Brown, donning an old "storm-beaten" hat, while playing the part of a fisherman. Brown "looked every way like a man of the neighborhood," wrote Douglass, "and as much at home as any of the farmers around there." Since his Kansas days, Brown had grown a thick gray beard and taken the alias Issac Smith to conceal his identity. Brown, Douglass, Watson and several others took seats among the limestone and discussed the planned assault on Harpers Ferry.

"I at once opposed the measure with all the arguments at my command," Douglass wrote. "It would be an attack upon the federal government, and would array the whole country against us." Brown answered that "rousing" was "just what the nation needed" and remained defiant as ever. He even begged Douglass to join him, giving the famous orator a bear hug and declaring, "Come with me, Douglass; I will defend you with my life." With a heavy heart, Douglass declined and returned home. He felt Brown's plan was "weak and broken," ill conceived and destined for failure.[220] It would be the last time he would see John Brown alive.

BROWN'S OCTOBER 16–18, 1859 assault on Harpers Ferry ended in tragedy. It was poorly planned, and as a result, the support he had expected from local African Americans never materialized. U.S. Marines soon arrived on the scene, surrounding Brown and his men. Outnumbered and outgunned, he and most of his party were captured, and Brown would be hanged for treason and murder in December.

Owen Brown, one of the abolitionist's many sons, awaited news of the attack in Sharpsburg, Maryland. Although he could hear firing in the distance, the devastation was not revealed to him until John E. Cook, one of his father's party, arrived. "Our men are all killed but seven," he murmured, telling Owen (errantly) that his father was among the dead. "Then he told us particulars," recalled Owen, "how the little band of seventeen whites and five blacks had surprised and taken the town and the armory, and held it, fighting all day long, but how at last companies amounting to eight hundred men had come in… guarding all the bridges and every route in or out." Cook urged that "[t]he best and only thing for us to do…was to make good our escape."

In doing so, Brown's associates would rely on the same Underground Railroad networks and methods that had aided fugitive slaves to freedom for years. Owen Brown recalled the necessity of "traveling only at night upon the edges of the clearings; sleeping and hiding by day in the

Donning a thick white beard, John Brown (or "Isaac Smith") hoped to evade detection as he planned his Harpers Ferry raid. This is how Brown appeared to residents of Chambersburg during the summer of 1859. *Library of Congress.*

thickets on the uninhabited mountain-tops; shunning all traveled roads at all times, except as we were obliged to cross them in the night; building no fires; buying or stealing no provisions; in fact, not speaking aloud till we should, at least, get beyond Chambersburg."

There, after considerable discussion, they again sought out Mary Ritner's boardinghouse. "I told the boys," recalled Owen, "that it was not fair to expose Mrs. Ritner. She had probably disavowed any knowledge of us, and it would be very easy to get her into trouble, without benefiting ourselves." However, he was outvoted by others in the group. It proved to be a dangerous decision. In the early dawn hours, they tapped on her second-story window with a bean pole. "Leave, leave!" she responded in a "frightened whisper," telling the men, "I couldn't help you if you were starving....The house is guarded by armed men!" Hurrying off, the group made their way to a thicket outside Chambersburg. There, local operatives provided the party with food until they were moved north to Bells Mills (near Punxsutawney), where "some person under the direction of Dr. Rutherford of Harrisburg" met the group and assisted them to safety.[221]

John Cook, who had lost touch with Owen Brown and the others before reaching Chambersburg, met a different fate. Daniel Logan, Franklin County's feared slave catcher, had seen a $1,000 reward for Cook's capture. Logan just happened to be at the Mount Alto Iron Furnace, where he was conversing with a friend, when Cook, "in his wanderings in search of food," stumbled out of a "mountain-thicket into an open space" within fifty yards of Logan. Recognizing Cook instantly, Logan's combined "hatred of the John Brown raiders" and "desire for the reward" spurred him to action.

Attempting to make the best of his gaffe, Cook walked boldly forward and introduced himself to Logan as a hunter seeking "to replenish his stock of bread and bacon." Logan responded warmly and suggested he follow him to his store (Logan, although very creative, did not own a store). Cook, letting down his guard, fell in behind Logan and his friend, who soon seized their opportunity, "grasped his arms and held him as in a vice." Thrown into a carriage, a bewildered Cook found himself going full speed south. He pleaded unsuccessfully with Logan for his freedom and was sent back to Virginia, where he, along with John Brown, would hang for their October raid.[222]

Osborne Perry Anderson and Albert Hazlett, also involved in Brown's plot, found themselves fleeing through the same region. Like Cook, they were up against the same organized "gang" of Cumberland Valley slave catchers who had been thwarting runaway slaves' bids for freedom for decades. Hazlett was given a carriage ride by a stranger but aroused suspicions with "a bundle in his hand which appeared to be a gun wrapped in a blanket." Like Owen Brown, he, too, went to Ritner's East King Street boardinghouse, but in broad daylight. Locals watched his every movement with apprehension. Ritner gave him lunch but warned that all eyes were already on her boardinghouse. "He went out the back door," recalled daughter Emma Ritner, "through the garden, tore a board off the fence, threw his gun down covering it with the board." Although Hazlett managed to leave Chambersburg, a posse of local men captured him on his way to Carlisle. He, too, would face extradition and ultimately the noose.[223]

More fortunate was Anderson, one of Brown's black associates. Anderson was none too sanguine about escaping through southern Pennsylvania, a region plagued by "the cupidity of the pro-slavery classes," which, he wrote, "would induce" locals "to seize a stranger on suspicion, or to go hunting for our party, so tempting to them is the bribe offered by the Slave Power." Traveling at night "as much as possible," he arrived in Chambersburg a few days later around 2:00 a.m., knocking at "the house of an acquaintance [possibly Henry Watson], who arose and let me in." "My appearance caused my friend to become greatly agitated," Anderson recalled. Even old friends feared the legal ramifications of what had taken place at Harpers Ferry. "I represented to him my famished condition, and told him I would leave as soon as I should be able to eat a morsel." However, just as he was preparing to leave, a U.S. marshal knocked at the front door. Anderson escaped out the back as the house was being searched. He moved east, likely connecting with Gettysburg operatives on his way to York. There, he was placed on the Pennsylvania Railroad to Philadelphia, ultimately reaching Canada.[224]

Abolitionists remained divided over Brown's use of violence. "Any one who believes that Slavery is right must logically regard John Brown as a robber and a brigand," declared James Freeman Clarke, a New England abolitionist. "But those who believe Slavery wrong; who justify the American Revolution; who admire Washington for contending with sword and fire against the government of Britain to free an oppressed people…must believe John Brown to be a hero, and the martyr to a principle."[225]

New Hampshire abolitionist Edwin M. Wheelock told listeners that he would support abolition "without shedding a drop of blood; but if that cannot be," the slaveholders bore the "guilt of the fierce conflict that must follow." If a peaceful solution could not be reached, Wheelock declared it the North's duty to intervene by "breaking every yoke" of bondage.[226] Not all abolitionists embraced Brown's legacy. Many sought to distance themselves.

Gerrit Smith, a wealthy philanthropist and abolitionist in Peterboro, New York, had a mental collapse. Having supported Brown financially in the past, Smith was overcome with guilt, feeling he had enabled the bloodshed. Within three weeks of the raid, he was committed to the New York State Asylum for the Insane. Frederick Douglass, fearing he might be arrested for his prior knowledge of Brown's plans, fled to Canada and later Europe.[227] Although Mary Ritner was also careful not to associate herself too closely with Brown in public, her sympathies remained in his corner. "I remember how loyal mother was to John Brown," recalled her daughter. "If anyone said he was a fanatic or a mono-maniac she was indignant."[228]

The nation, too, was polarized over Brown's actions. The Democratic Chambersburg *Valley Spirit* called his raid an "attempt to subvert the Government of the United States by a handful of crazy fanatics," which was "only the beginning—the foreshadowing of more serious troubles." Brown, they claimed, had inspired slave populations to rise up and commit "rapine and murder at our own firesides." Abolitionists, "so blinded by their political prejudices" and "seditious principles," bore "the awful responsibility for this state of things," the paper claimed.

The paper's proslavery editor was disgusted that Brown and his men had used Chambersburg as a staging area. "Our community has by some means, of which we were entirely unaware, become mixed up with this insurrection. While we were harbouring, for months these desperadoes among us we do not believe that a single one of our white citizen was in any way connected with them, or even suspected their designs." Ultimately, he asserted that blame lay with the town's black populace. "In regard to our blacks it is believed that a portion of them knew the object of these men, were associated with them, and would have joined them if successful. There is no sympathy in this community for the fugitives, and if any of them should come this way they will receive no assistance or protection from our citizens."[229] Its rival paper, the now-Republican *Franklin Repository*, argued that Brown had "infuriate[d] the zeal of the slave power" and awakened the northern people. The paper opined:

> And what is it that is thus on trial before the great public of these United States?—What is it that is undergoing the scrutiny of thousands of eager eyes? What is it that will be hung up on the gallows in the gaze of all men? Not John Brown, but Slavery! John Brown had already received the verdict of the people as a brave and honest man.....Not John Brown but Slavery will be gibbeted, when he hangs upon the gallows.—Slavery itself

Gerrit Smith, a noted abolitionist and philanthropist from Peterboro, New York, was racked with guilt in the wake of John Brown's raid. *Library of Congress.*

will receive the scorn and execration it has invoked for him. That execution will strength[en] and consolidate the feeling of the North in determined and irrepressible hatred of the barbarism that makes traitors and criminals of men who seek to deliver the oppressed. Just this was needed to arouse the North to the perils that threaten the nation from the preponderance of the slave power in the Federal Administration….When John Brown is executed, it will be seen that he has done his work even more effectually than if he had succeeded in running of a few hundred slaves.[230]

This "brief inauguration of a reign of terror was needed, to prepare the way for the peaceful but triumphant revolution by the ballot-box which shall wrest the government ordained for liberty, from the tyranny that has usurped it," the *Repository* confidently assured its readers.[231] As the election of 1860 ramped up, slavery remained the central issue. The *Valley Spirit* continued its attacks on abolition, arguing in a column addressed to the "Merchants and Manufacturers of the North" that anti-southern sentiment would cost them business.[232] The paper printed articles titled "Save Us from Abolitionism," in which editors made often dubious claims in an effort to tap into anti-black sentiment. On the eve of the election, the *Valley Spirit* asserted that white women were being married off in large numbers to black men in Massachusetts.[233]

Abolitionists endured these attacks and in November 1860 helped elect Abraham Lincoln as the sixteenth president of the United States. In a four-way race, Lincoln won only 40 percent of the popular vote, running on a platform of containing slavery to where it already existed. Although they were successful at the polls, abolitionists would first have to win a civil war and sway their president to a more aggressive approach in order to finally abolish slavery.

"NOT A SLAVE BENEATH ITS FOLD"

ABOLITIONISTS' FINAL EFFORT

T he Union Safe!" read the first handbill in Gettysburg announcing Abraham Lincoln's election to the presidency in November 1860. "The returns come in slowly from the district. There have been large gains for Lincoln. His majority will probably reach 100 in the County! OLD ABE IS PRESIDENT!"[234]

A few weeks later, South Carolina became the first state to secede from the Union. It cited "an increasing hostility on the part of the non-slaveholding States to the Institution of Slavery" and "the election of a man to the high office of President of the United States whose opinions and purposes are hostile to slavery." The North was acting under a "current of anti-slavery feeling," which had led it astray from its "constitutional obligation" to return escaped southern slaves.[235]

Other southern states followed. "Our position is thoroughly identified with the institution of slavery—the greatest material interest of the world," declared delegates at Mississippi's Secession convention. Slave-produced products "have become necessities of the world, and a blow at slavery is a blow at commerce and civilization. That blow has been long aimed at the institution, and was at the point of reaching its consummation. There was no choice left us but submission to the mandates of abolition, or a dissolution of the Union, whose principles had been subverted to work out our ruin."[236]

In Chambersburg, editors of the *Valley Spirit* blamed the war on abolitionists. "Northern fanaticism rules the hour—sectional hate and abolition rage have goaded the South" to secession. "Has it come to this that we must be forced

This handbill, circulated in Gettysburg, bore the first news of Lincoln's election. For local abolitionists, the election of an antislavery man to the White House represented a major shift in political tides. *J. Howard Wert Gettysburg Collection.*

to remain in an abolition confederacy and consider negroes our equals?" the paper complained.[237]

Five months later, the first shots were fired at Charleston Harbor, South Carolina. When President Lincoln called for seventy-five thousand volunteers to suppress the rebellion, local colleges packed with northern and southern students were soon struggling to keep their tutelages in the classrooms. "The excitement which has arisen from the sudden outbreak of the war has been fully shared by the students of the College," noted Herman Merrills Johnson, the new president of Dickinson College. Annoyed, he complained that "[q]uite a number have gone home; some at the call of their parents; some, from a supposed necessity; some, procuring the consent of their parents by a representation, prompted by the first hasty impulse and by an exaggerated estimate of impending danger; and some, embracing the pretext for relief from the tedium of study." Many southern students left, either to join the Confederate armies or fearing retaliation from the surrounding community.[238]

Dickinson student James Patterson recalled dispassionately shaking hands with his southern classmates, "bidding farewell without emotion, but fully understanding each was going to support the views he had espoused." Patterson, who joined the 148th Pennsylvania Infantry, would encounter

Left: Southerner David Stone, Dickinson College class of 1859. *Archives and Special Collections, Dickinson College.*

Right: After graduating from Dickinson, Stone joined the Confederate army. Here he is pictured in 1863, donning his Confederate uniform. Stone would ultimately be captured on the battlefield by Patterson, who subsequently married Stone's sister. *Archives and Special Collections, Dickinson College.*

and capture his former roommate, David D. Stone of Norfolk, Virginia, at the Battle of Spotsylvania in May 1864.[239] As if their strange meeting was not enough, Stone later married Patterson's sister Isabel, and the former roommates, enemy combatants and brothers-in-law served as co-principals of the Tuscarora Academy after the war.[240]

Not all were so exuberant. "The sectional strife, arising chiefly from the unfortunate contest about slavery, has culminated," lamented Abraham Essick, a Lutheran minister in Franklin County. "Our lot has been cast in calamitous times, and we who are near the confines of slave and free territory will, doubtless, be the greatest suffered."[241]

From Carlisle, Dickinson president Johnson wrote Lincoln to express his support. Johnson was regarded by northern students and locals as a firm Union man with antislavery principles.[242] "The National heart was benumbed & the national conscience perverted on the subject which is the immediate cause of the terrible calamity now upon us," he penned, speaking of slavery. "The people," Johnson continued, had been led to believe that the rights of slaveholders "were before all other interest[s] of a great & Christian nation....But the hour passes." The "conviction" to see slavery as a moral evil "has arrived," Johnson proclaimed. "And if your Excellency could publish an order tomorrow that should remove the cornerstone of the great fabric of slavery & let the temple tumble in ruins...it would meet with a hearty response form nine tenths...of the truly loyal people north & south."

However, Johnson's subsequent lines made clear the issue of emancipation—even among abolitionists—was no simple matter. "[I]f by the magic of a word the shackles of four million slaves could be loosened...we are but fairly face to face with the great problem your Excellency is laboring to solve—what shall be done with the negro free[.]" Johnson noted that former masters would likely be abusive of freedmen, and in "the free North they are even less welcome....We may go further & say that this grievance will not be mitigated by time; but will be constantly aggravated instead; that such is the inevitable law of society, where two races [ex]ist together in the same country, so unlike in blood & manner so as to forbid a coalescence into a homogenous people. The only alternative then, is colonization. We are shut up to that conclusion."

Johnson proposed resettling freed slaves on "the peninsula of Florida, & the low country of Georgia & South Carolina." He had no sympathy over confiscating the land of slaveholders. He considered slave owners not only the instigators of the war but also disloyal for seceding. "No loyal tear would drop," he wrote, "no loyal breath would utter a sigh."[243]

WHILE JOHNSON PONDERED THE war's ultimate end, other local abolitionists were eager to participate. Near Gettysburg, the five stout sons of James McAllister, who had spent their boyhoods working on the Underground, all enlisted in the Union army.

At nineteen, Theodore, who had come of age listening to the fugitives' haunting tales during the 1850s, left home shortly after the Union defeat at First Manassas in July 1861. He was met by "my dear old mother, with some of the blood of Robert Burns coursing through her veins and with tears washing her face," who told him: "I could see you go with less of sorrow if the Government you are going to help save did not sanction slavery." Theodore replied, "Mother, if I am spared to return to you I do not believe there will be any slaves living under our flag." His father, "with a pause and drooping head," murmured, "Mother, do not say anything more, the boy has caught a glimpse of why this terrible war came upon us." Suddenly straightening "to his full stature and with [a] flashing eye," betraying the passion he had first articulated some twenty-five years earlier, McAllister

A recent Pennsylvania College graduate, J. Howard Wert, son of abolitionist Adam Wert, served in the 209th Pennsylvania Infantry, one of many "fighting abolitionists" from South Central Pennsylvania. *J. Howard Wert Gettysburg Collection.*

directed his son: "Sad as our hearts are at this parting, I am going to say to you, 'Go, and may God bless and keep you.'"

For the McAllister family and countless other abolitionists, the Civil War was the ultimate struggle in the fight for emancipation. The public meetings attended, the aid given to fugitives in the dark of night, the insults endured—all had amounted to this pivotal moment. Although many northerners maintained the conflict was a war to "preserve the Union," abolitionists

The son of a Fayetteville abolitionist, Samuel Wiley Crawford commanded a division of Pennsylvania Reserves at the Battle of Gettysburg. *Library of Congress.*

thought otherwise. Theodore McAllister viewed the war as an opportunity to realize the "true" promise of the "land of the free."

Theodore would live to see his parents again, as would his brothers Samuel and Calvin, who served in the Twenty-First Pennsylvania Cavalry. Another brother, John McAllister, saw action in the Eighty-Seventh Pennsylvania Infantry. Not all the McAllisters, however, would survive the conflict. His older brother James "Aleck"—the same young lad who in 1849 had helped Adam Wert's son conceal a fugitive in a rocky hideout— had gone west before the war broke out. He enlisted in an Illinois regiment and was killed in action in July 1863 near Vicksburg, Mississippi—the same time Confederates were fighting over his old family homestead.[244]

Another mile to the southeast, the son of Adam Wert, J. Howard, now in his early twenties, obtained a special commission to recruit U.S. Colored Troops from the Gettysburg area.[245] His efforts, however, were interrupted by the climactic three-day battle that raged around him. In the days and weeks that followed, the fields, farmhouses, barns and churches of his childhood would be filled with wounded and dying soldiers.

The son of another local abolitionist, Dr. Samuel Crawford—the agent of "Crawford's Lane" in Fayetteville—rose to prominence as a Union general. Raised in an abolitionist household, Samuel Wylie Crawford followed his father's footsteps, attending medical school and joining the army as a surgeon. Crawford was present at Fort Sumter when the first shots of the war rang out. In July 1863, Crawford was back in Pennsylvania, serving as a brigadier general at Gettysburg.[246]

Before the Confederate army reached his Caledonia Ironworks in western Adams County, Thaddeus Stevens had journeyed there personally on horseback, retrieving vital paperwork and documents.[247] He knew the price he was about to pay. The rank and file of the Confederate army loathed Stevens, a man they knew as a "mean abolitionist" and harsh critic of the southern way of life. Upon reaching "a very large rolling mill and iron mines belonging to Thadius [*sic*] Stevens," a Louisiana soldier wrote with pleasure, "[w]e destroyed his mills and mines by burning."[248]

Many Confederates sought to settle the score with Pennsylvania abolitionists, who had been steadily weakening the slave system for decades. In western Cumberland County, southern cavalrymen questioned locals "if there were any abolitionists about here."[249] The home of Richard Woods, an abolitionist who lived southwest of Carlisle, was also searched by Confederates. However, Woods and most of the free blacks working in his employ had already fled east of the river.[250]

By far, the region's African American residents suffered the most. Heading the vanguard of Robert E. Lee's army, Brigadier General Albert G. Jenkins of Virginia and his brigade of Virginia cavalry captured countless free blacks as "contraband," or spoils of war. While in Franklin County, one local watched Jenkins's mounted troopers "scouring the fields about town and searching" for "Negroes....Many of them were caught after a desperate chase and being fired at[.]" Although in Greencastle several white citizens pleaded on the behalf of captured blacks, securing the release of a few, most were not so fortunate.[251]

After the battle, many local blacks found the "new birth of freedom" President Lincoln spoke so famously of on November 19, but not in the way the sixteenth president would have expected. His farm ruined by the battle, Underground Railroad conductor Basil Biggs was among those reinterring bodies into the National Cemetery, which Lincoln dedicated with his Gettysburg Address.[252] Blacks from as far away as Chambersburg came to Gettysburg, making fifty cents per day identifying and reinterring bodies. "Some of them had [paper identification] tags," members of a Chambersburg family recalled. "Sometimes the tags were shot off and they didn't know who they were. They would gather these soldiers up and put them in a certain place." The work was exhausting. One worker "had to put a cloth soaked in turpentine over his mouth."

The Confederate invasion of 1863 had precipitated a mass exodus of blacks from South Central Pennsylvania. Some left ahead of the southern columns, never to return; others, like Biggs, came back and remained pivotal members of the African American community for decades. Still others returned temporarily, saving money as they worked reinterring bodies, later using their savings to move to Canada.[253]

Ten miles to the north, at Yellow Hill, Samuel and Nelson, sons of Edward and Annie Mathews, enlisted in the U.S. Colored Troops. Their younger brother, William, only fourteen years of age, ran away from home to join his brothers in the war. All three would survive the war, but unspecified injuries plagued William for the rest of his life.[254] They were no doubt encouraged by Frederick Douglass, who had returned from England to push for the inclusion of black soldiers. "The chance is now given you to end in a day the bondage of centuries," he told prospective recruits in March 1863, "and to rise…to the place of common equality with all other varieties of men. Remember," Douglass implored the men, "who followed noble John Brown, and fell as glorious martyrs for the cause of the slave. Remember that in a contest with oppression, the Almighty has no attribute which can take sides with oppressors."[255]

Others played different but nonetheless crucial roles. By the time of the Civil War, John McClintock, formerly the abolitionist professor at Dickinson College, was an ocean away. From the American chapel in Paris, the Methodist scholar sought to stymie anti-Union sentiment brewing in both France and England. With the fear of foreign intervention to help the Confederacy, McClintock set about convincing his European colleagues of the justness of the Union cause—namely, that slavery must be abolished.[256]

In Congress, Gettysburg's former state representative, Thaddeus Stevens (now a congressman from Lancaster), labored to secure the passage of the

From Paris, former Dickinson College professor John McClintock defended the Union's motives for civil war and tamed prospects of European support for the Confederacy. *Archives and Special Collections, Dickinson College.*

As a congressman from Lancaster, Thaddeus Stevens exerted considerable influence in the drafting of the Thirteenth Amendment. With the war's end, he came to embody the "Radical Republicans" of the North, who sought to give rights of citizenship and voting to previously disenfranchised southern blacks. *Library of Congress.*

Laus Deo!

[ON HEARING THE BELLS RING FOR THE CONSTI-
TUTIONAL AMENDMENT ABOLISHING SLAVERY
IN THE UNITED STATES!]

BY JOHN G. WHITTIER.

It is done!
Clang of bell and roar of gun
Send the tidings up and down.
How the belfries rock and reel,
How the great guns, peal on peal,
Fling the joy from town to town!

Ring, O bells!
Every stroke exultant tells
Of the burial hour of crime.
Loud and long that all may hear,
Ring for every listening ear
Of Eternity and Time!

Let us kneel:
God's own voice is in that peal,
And this spot is holy ground.
Lord forgive us! What are we,
That our eyes this glory see,
That our ears have heard the sound!

For the Lord
On the whirlwind is abroad;
In the earthquake He has spoken;
He has smitten with his thunder
The iron walls asunder,
And the gates of brass are broken!

Loud and long,
Lift the old exulting song;
Sing with Miriam by the sea:
He hath cast the mighty down;
Horse and rider sink and drown;
He hath triumphed gloriously!

Did we dare
In our agony of prayer
Ask for more than He has done!
When was ever His right hand
Over any time or land
Stretched as now beneath the sun!

How they pale,
Ancient myth, and song, and tale,
In this wonder of our days,
When the cruel rod of war
Blossoms white with righteous law,
And the wrath of man is praise!

Blotted out!
All within and all about
Shall a fresher life begin;
Freer breathe the universe
As it rolls its heavy curse
On the dead and buried sin!

It is done!
In the circuit of the sun
Shall the sound thereof go forth.
It shall bid the sad rejoice,
It shall give the dumb a voice,
It shall belt with joy the earth!

Thirteenth Amendment, long the dream of abolitionists. Not only would the amendment prohibit slavery throughout the United States and all its territories, but it would also give shape and meaning to a war that had ravaged the nation and taken hundreds of thousands of lives. His former law student and Gettysburg native Edward McPherson, following his 1862 reelection defeat, stayed in Washington as the House clerk and remained Stevens's confidant. Another member of Stevens's inner circle was the Adams County–born housekeeper and assistant Lydia Hamilton Smith.

In January 1865, the House finally ratified the Thirteenth Amendment, and the trio—all with strong ties to South Central Pennsylvania—rejoiced. Smith clipped a poem titled "Laus Deo!" ("Praise be to God"), penned by John Greenleaf Whittier "on hearing the bells ring for the Constitutional Amendment abolishing slavery in the United States!"[257] The proud moment was the culmination of a great social, moral and religious struggle.

After decades of campaigning, the victory of complete abolition stunned even those who had labored their entire lives in the cause. Just several years earlier, recalled Frederick Douglass, "slavery seemed to be at the very top of its power;

Exulting over the Thirteenth Amendment's passage, the Adams County–born Lydia Hamilton Smith clipped this poem by John Greenleaf Whittier for her own personal use. *J. Howard Wert Gettysburg Collection.*

the national government, with all its powers and appliances, was in its hands, and it bade fair to wield them for many years to come. Nobody could then see that in the short space of four years this power would be broken and the slave system destroyed."[258]

"Is it any wonder that I did all that I could to keep 'Old Glory' floating over all our broad land, and to wipe a horrible dark stain from its folds?" Gettysburg's Theodore McAllister later wrote of his war service. "And I carried aloft in my own brawny hands our own proud banner as we marched homeward, after every hostile gun was stacked…and not a slave beneath its fold."[259]

NOTES

Prologue

1. Jefferson, *Notes on the State of Virginia*, 169–71.
2. Thomas Jefferson, autobiography draft fragment, July 27, 1821, Jefferson Papers, Library of Congress.
3. Ibid.
4. Rohrbough, *Land Office Business*, 103, 126, 212–13, 218.
5. Gideon Fitz, quoted in Rohrbough, *Land Office Business*, 212.
6. *Fort Claiborne Courier*, quoted in, Rohrbough, *Land Office Business*, 126.
7. DeBow, *Statistical View of the United States*, 145–47, 149–50; Phillips, *American Negro Slavery*, 183–86, 332–33, 391; Phillips, *Life and Labor in the Old South*, 110–11.
8. Thomas Jefferson to St. George Tucker, August 28, 1797, and Thomas Jefferson to John Holmes, April 22, 1820, Jefferson Papers, Library of Congress.
9. John Calhoun, "On the Commercial Treaty with Great Britain," 29 Annals of Cong. 531-532 (1816).
10. [Fox], *Gospel Family Order*, 16, 18.
11. Lay, *All Slave-Keepers*, 29, 43.
12. Soderlund and Wood, "Notes and Documents," 177–95.
13. Gummere, *Journal and Essays of John Woolman*, 161–62.
14. Sassi, "With a Little Help from the Friends," 33–40.
15. Churchman, *Account of the Gospel Labours*, 175–76.

16. Sassi, "With a Little Help from the Friends," 33–47.

17. Sinha, *Slave's Cause*, 21.

18. Sassi, "With a Little Help from the Friends," 33–47; Clarkson, *History of the Rise*, 118.

19. Nash and Soderlund, *Freedom by Degrees*, 4–5, 71, 89.

20. Lewis, Underground Railroad memoirs, RG 5/087, Series 1, Box 1.

21. "Letter from Bishop Allen," *New York Freedom's Journal*, November 2, 1827; Richard S. Newman, *The Transformation of American Abolitionism: Fighting Slavery in the Early Republic* (Chapel Hill: University of North Carolina Press, 2002), 86–95.

Chapter 1

22. Coffin, *Reminiscences of Levi Coffin*, 12–13; Howe, *Historical Collections of Virginia*, 407–17.

23. Seward, *William H. Seward*, 1:265–272.

24. Hundley, *Social Relations*, 139–41.

25. Earle, *Life, Travels, and Opinions of Benjamin Lundy*, 13–15.

26. Lundy, quoted in Dillon, *Benjamin Lundy*, 6–7.

27. Ibid., 15–19.

28. For quotations and an excellent summary of the opening debates, see Moore, *Missouri Controversy*, 33–49, 52–54, 59–63.

29. Dillon, *Benjamin Lundy*, 19.

30. Sinha, *Slave's Cause*, 187.

31. Cobb and Tallmadge, quoted in Moore, *Missouri Controversy*, 50.

32. Randolph, quoted in Moore, *Missouri Controversy*, 93.

33. Thomas Jefferson to John Holmes, April 22, 1820, Thomas Jefferson Papers, Library of Congress.

34. Benjamin Lundy to Andrew Jackson, September 4, 1823, Andrew Jackson Papers, Library of Congress; Dillon, *Benjamin Lundy*, 40–41.

35. Dillon, *Benjamin Lundy*, 48.

36. Lundy, quoted in Dillon, *Benjamin Lundy*, 49.

37. Dillon, *Benjamin Lundy*, 71, 76–77.

38. Ibid., 79–89.

39. Ibid., 109–27; Anadolu-Okur, *Dismantling Slavery*, 1–21.

40. Dillon, *Benjamin Lundy*, 109–27; Anadolu-Okur, *Dismantling Slavery*, 1–21; Remini, *Andrew Jackson*, 1–37.

41. American Convention for Promoting the Abolition of Slavery, *Minutes of the Adjourned Session*, 3–10.

42. Lydia Shotwell Lundy to Halliday Jackson, December 7, 1828, Halliday Jackson Letterbook, Swarthmore College.

43. Benjamin Lundy to Lydia Lundy Wierman, May 29, 1831, in Armstrong, *Lundy Family*, 381–83.

44. Wert, *Episodes of Gettysburg*, 92–93.

45. Joel Wierman to Adam Wert, August 6, 1837, J. Howard Wert Gettysburg Collection.

46. Smedley, *History of the Underground Railroad*, 40, 43–44; Lewis, Underground Railroad memoirs, Series 1, Box 1.

47. May, *Some Recollections of Our Antislavery Conflict*, 91–97.

48. Lydia Shotwell Lundy to Halliday Jackson, June 20, 1828, Jackson Letterbook, Swarthmore College.

49. Huldah Justice to Adam Wert, August 16, 1837, J. Howard Wert Gettysburg Collection.

Chapter 2

50. "To Be Sold," *Kline's Carlisle Weekly Gazette*, May 21, 1794; Bureau of the Census, *Aggregate Amount of Each Description of Persons*, 39–41; Bureau of the Census, *Census for 1820*, 87–93; Bureau of the Census, *Abstract of the Returns of the Fifth Census*, 12–13.

51. Cazenove, *Cazenove Journal 1794*, 67.

52. *Carlisle American Volunteer*, April 24, 1823.

53. John Peck, Cumberland County Tax Records, 1823, 1829, 1844, microfilm at CCHS.

54. "Repent and Be Converted," *Friend of Man*, September 6, 1837.

55. "Using the Products of Slave Labor," *Spirit of Liberty*, December 11, 1841.

56. [Austin], *Remarks on Dr. Channing's Slavery*, 46.

57. *Proceedings of the Rhode Island Anti-Slavery Convention*, 57.

58. *Proceedings of the Ohio Anti-Slavery Convention*, 51.

59. *Proceedings of the N.H. Anti-Slavery Convention*, 34.

60. *Proceedings of the New England Anti-Slavery Convention*, 20–21.

61. "Why We Should Have a Paper," *Colored American*, March 4, 1837.

62. "Difficulties of Abolition," *Colored American*, May 27, 1837.

63. Bigelow, "Antebellum Ohio's Black Barbers," 26–40.

64. Anadolu-Okur, *Dismantling Slavery*, 23–33.

65. Ibid., 34–36.
66. Garrison and Garrison, *William Lloyd Garrison*, 1:225.
67. "Speech of J. Miller McKim," *Proceedings of the American Anti-Slavery Society*, 31–33.
68. "Agents for the Advocate," *Weekly Advocate*, January 7, 1837.
69. McKim, *Sketch of the Slave Trade*, 5–8.
70. Brown, "Miller McKim," 59–62.
71. Freeman, Pickard and Woodwell, *Whittier and Whittierland*, 39–40.
72. Lewis, Underground Railroad memoirs, Series 1, Box 1.
73. *Proceedings of the Pennsylvania Convention*, 7.
74. Ibid., 9.
75. Freeman, Pickard and Woodwell, *Whittier and Whittierland*, 39–40; May, *Some Recollections of Our Antislavery Conflict*, 82–91.
76. *Proceedings of the Pennsylvania Convention*, 5.
77. Ibid., 7.
78. Ibid., 12, 22, 29–43.
79. Joseph T. Kelly, quoted in Harrold, *Subversives*, 3; Jane Grey Swisshelm to Horace Greely, April 10, 1850, quoted in Harrold, *Subversives*, 3; DeBow, *Statistical View of the United States*, 192; Dickens, *American Notes*, 1:146.
80. Martineau, *Retrospect of Western Travel*, 1:235–73.
81. DeBow, *Statistical View of the United States*, 63, 82.
82. *Proceedings of the Pennsylvania Convention*, 62–64.
83. "Address of the Massachusetts Liberty State Committee," September 9, 1846, quoted in Harrold, *Subversives*, 5.
84. *Third Annual Report of the American Anti-Slavery Society*, 54–55.
85. *Proceedings of the Pennsylvania Convention*, 92–93.

Chapter 3

86. *Adams Centinel*, November 22, 1820.
87. J. Howard Wert, "Old Time Notes of Adams County: Tramps!" *Gettysburg Star & Sentinel*, November 21, 1906.
88. *Star & Republican Banner*, November 30, 1835; Hoch, *Thaddeus Stevens*, 236.
89. *Gettysburg Star & Republican Banner*, July 11, 1836; Minutes of the Adams County Anti-Slavery Society, December 3, 1836, J. Howard Wert Gettysburg Collection.
90. *Gettysburg Star & Republican Banner*, September 26, 1836.

91. Wert, *Episodes of Gettysburg*, 30–34.

92. Minutes of the Adams County Anti-Slavery Society, December 3, 1836, J. Howard Wert Gettysburg Collection.

93. *Proceedings of the Pennsylvania Convention*, 7.

94. J. Howard Wert, "Old Time Notes of Adams County: A Bold Declaration of Principles," *Gettysburg Star & Sentinel*, April 19, 1905.

95. Joel Wierman to Adam Wert, August 6, 1837, J. Howard Wert Gettysburg Collection.

96. Minutes of the Adams County Anti-Slavery Society, December 2, 1837, J. Howard Wert Gettysburg Collection.

97. *Conscience versus Cotton*, 1–10.

98. [Austin], *Remarks on Dr. Channing's Slavery*, 39.

99. William Reynolds to Adam Wert, n.d., J. Howard Wert Gettysburg Collection.

100. Minutes of the Adams County Anti-Slavery Society, December 30, 1837, J. Howard Wert Gettysburg Collection.

101. Minutes of meeting held at Carlisle, December 29, 1836, MG 72, Folder 1a, CCHS. Among the notable figures to sign this petition was Judge Frederick Watts, an influential Carlisle native who later served as president of the Cumberland Valley Railroad.

102. *Gettysburg Star & Republican Banner*, March 13, 1837; "Remarks of Mr. Blanchard," *Gettysburg Star & Republican Banner*, April 17, 1837.

103. *Gettysburg Star & Republican Banner*, March 20, 1837; "Mr. Cooper's Remarks," *Gettysburg Star & Republican Banner*, May 29, 1837; Jonathan Blanchard, "Hon. Thaddeus Stevens," *Christian Cynosure*, April 5, 1883; Jonathan Blanchard, "Hon. Thaddeus Stevens," *Christian Cynosure*, April 5, 1883.

104. *Gettysburg Star & Republican Banner*, March 20, 1837; Blanchard, "Personal Recollections," *Christian Cynosure*, December 29, 1868; Blanchard, "Hon. Thaddeus Stevens," *Christian Cynosure*, April 5, 1883.

105. *Memorial Addresses*, 52–53.

106. Foner, *Frederick Douglass*, 551.

107. James Miller McKim to Adam Wert, March 30, 1845, J. Howard Wert Gettysburg Collection.

108. Benjamin S. Jones to Adam Wert, April 7, 1845, J. Howard Wert Gettysburg Collection.

109. Clerk of the House of Representatives, *Abstract of the Returns of the Fifth Census*, 12–13.

110. Smith, *On the Edge of Freedom*, 22–23, 38; Wert, *Episodes of Gettysburg*, 27.

111. *Gettysburg Star & Republican Banner*, April 9, 1839; Hiram E. Wertz, "A Paper Read on 'The Underground Railway' before the Hamilton Library Association, of Carlisle, Penna., on the evening of the 24th of February 1911," typescript, MG 72, Folder 7a, CCHS; Hoch, *Thaddeus Stevens in Gettysburg*, 236, 243–44.

112. Kaplan, *John Quincy Adams*, 490–91; *Congressional Globe*, 24th Congress, 1st Session, 498–99.

113. Minutes of the Adams County Anti-Slavery Society, December 30, 1837, J. Howard Wert Gettysburg Collection.

114. *Third Annual Report of the American Anti-Slavery Society*, 11.

115. *Proceedings of the New England Anti-Slavery Convention*, 13.

116. George Chambers to Adam Wert, January 30, 1837, J. Howard Wert Gettysburg Collection. A notice in the *Gettysburg Star & Republican Banner* on January 2, 1837, reads: "Persons holding petitions for the abolition of Slavery in the District of Columbia and the U.S. Territories, are requested to obtain as many names as possible and forward them without delay, either to this office, or to our Representative in Congress, the Hon. GEORGE CHAMBERS."

117. Joel Wierman to Adam Wert, August 6, 1837, J. Howard Wert Gettysburg Collection.

118. *Fifth Annual Report of the Board of Managers*, 42.

119. [Lundy], *War in Texas*, 3.

120. Daniel Sheffer to Adam Wert, January 9, 1838, J. Howard Wert Gettysburg Collection.

121. Daniel Sheffer to Adam Wert, May 14, 1838, J. Howard Wert Gettysburg Collection.

122. Allen Robinette to Adam Wert, January 27, 1839, J. Howard Wert Gettysburg Collection.

123. James Cooper to Adam Wert, June 4, 1840, J. Howard Wert Gettysburg Collection.

124. James Cooper to Adam Wert, January 18, 1841, J. Howard Wert Gettysburg Collection.

125. James Cooper to Adam Wert, February 14, 1842, J. Howard Wert Gettysburg Collection.

126. J. McAllister to Adam Wert, April 19, 1844, J. Howard Wert Gettysburg Collection.

127. *Adams Centinel*, June 5, 1805, July 25, 1810, September 16, 1818; Warner, Beers and Co., *History of Cumberland and Adams Counties*, 3:364–65; Pennsylvania Archives, Series 3, 21:740; *Biographical Congressional Directory*, 674–75.

128. McPherson, *Disunion Conspiracy*, 3; Thaddeus Stevens to Edward McPherson, October 30, 1862, McPherson to Stevens, October 31, 1862, in Palmer and Ochoa, *Selected Papers of Thaddeus Stevens*, 1:326–27.
129. "Slave's Refuge Society," *Pennsylvania Freeman*, February 2, 1841.
130. Sinha, *Slave's Cause*, 28.
131. Vermilyea, "Effect of Lee's Invasion"; Smith, *On the Edge of Freedom*, 28–29; A. Stanley Ulrich to J. Howard Wert, 1904, J. Howard Wert Scrapbook, J. Howard Wert Gettysburg Collection.
132. "Leading Colored Citizen," *Gettysburg Compiler*, June 11, 1906; McCauslin, *Yellow Hill*, 3–11.
133. "Certificate of Death," Lydia Hamilton Smith, February 14, 1884, Vital Records Division; Trefousse, *Thaddeus Stevens*, 69; Egerton, *Wars of Reconstruction*, 211.

Chapter 4

134. "Great Anti Abolition Meeting," *Franklin Repository*, April 18, 1837; Sharpe, *Memoir of George Chambers*, 20–22. Twenty-one years later, in 1858, the *Valley Spirit* in Chambersburg would reprint the entire proceedings as first reported in 1837, citing Chambers's name, proudly ranking him among "other prominent and patriotic citizens of your county, who as long as twenty one years ago published to the world their condemnation of the assaults of Abolitionists upon the institutions of the South—assaults now repeated, more violently than ever, by Black Republicans of Pennsylvania and of all the Northern States." See Chambersburg, *Valley Spirit*, August 11, 1858.
135. "The Slave Trade—Emancipation, &c.," *Franklin Repository*, November 13, 1827.
136. "Abolition," *Franklin Repository*, May 29, 1838.
137. *Valley Spirit*, March 30, 1859.
138. *Valley Spirit*, April 21, 1851.
139. Seilhamer, *Bard Family*, 226–31.
140. *Valley Spirit*, March 31, 1853. The *Spirit* refers to Gerrit Smith, a famous abolitionist from Peterboro, New York, and Harriet Beecher Stowe, author of the bestselling abolitionist novel *Uncle Tom's Cabin*.
141. *Valley Spirit*, November 18, 1852.
142. Bates and Richard, *History of Franklin County*, 321.
143. Ibid.
144. Drew, *North-Side View of Slavery*, 116.

145. *Valley Spirit*, April 21, 1851.

146. O.P. [Murray] to Jeremiah Zeamer, September 25, 1901, Zeamer Papers, File 40-9, Cumberland County Historical Society.

147. Interview with Larry Dean Calimer, b. 1938, in C. Bernard Ruffin, "Slavery, Civil War, and Emancipation," typescript in Underground Railroad file, Franklin County Historical Society; McClure, "Episode of John Brown's Raid," 279–87.

148. O.P. [Murray] to Jeremiah Zeamer, September 25, 1901, Zeamer Papers, File 40-9, Cumberland County Historical Society.

149. S.R. McAllister to J. Howard Wert, December 2, 1904, J. Howard Wert Gettysburg Collection; Smith, *On the Edge of Freedom*, 27–28.

150. Interview with Ida Mary Lewis, b. 1924, in Ruffin, *This Is My Story*, 408–14; interview with May Anderson Lewis, b. 1896, interview with Levantia Sellers Peyton, b. 1906, interview with Mary Jones Carter, b. 1902, in Ruffin, "Slavery, Civil War, and Emancipation," Franklin County Historical Society.

151. "The Mercersburg Affair," *Franklin Repository*, October 17, 1837.

152. *Franklin Repository*, July 27, 1830.

153. "From the Gettysburg Anti-Masonic Star," *Franklin Repository*, newspaper clippings, Underground Railroad file, Franklin County Historical Society. Blanchard's letter to Middleton is dated August 9, 1837.

154. Wertz, "A Paper Read on 'The Underground Railway,'" typescript, MG 72, Folder 7a, Cumberland County Historical Society.

155. "Some History of Black Gap; Was in Underground R.R.," *Chambersburg Public Opinion*, November 3, 1921.

156. O.P. [Murray] to Jeremiah Zeamer, September 25, 1901, Zeamer Papers, File 40-9, Cumberland County Historical Society; Sproull and Willson, *Reformed Presbyterian*, 14:355.

157. Anderson Family Exhibit, Allison-Antrim Museum, Greencastle, PA; Anderson, *Presbyterianism*, 155.

158. Seilhamer, *Biographical Annals of Franklin County*, 633; Kittochtinny Historical Society, *Papers Read before the Society*, 3:188.

159. Tritt and Watt, *At a Place Called the Boiling Springs*, 111–17.

160. Adeleke, *Without Regard to Race*, 21, 40–69. For more on Delany and Douglass's relationship and roles in the abolitionist movement, see Levine, *Martin Delany, Frederick Douglass*.

161. For further details, see Smith, *On the Edge of Freedom*, 154–56.

Chapter 5

162. Wingert, *Slavery and the Underground Railroad*, 26–27.

163. Newspaper clippings from 1788–89, *Pennsylvania Herald and York General Advertiser*, slavery file, York County Heritage Trust.

164. For a comprehensive account of York County's Underground Railroad network, see Mingus, *Ground Swallowed Them Up*, 23–49, 89–99.

165. Prowell, *History of York County*, 1:596.

166. Ibid., 1:597.

167. Ibid., 1:594.

Chapter 6

168. William Frederic Worner, "The Columbia Race Riots," in *Papers Read before the Lancaster County Historical Society, Friday, October 6, 1922* (Lancaster, PA: Lancaster Historical Society, 1922), 175–81; Smedley, *History of the Underground Railroad in Chester and the Neighboring Counties*, 28.

169. Worner, "The Columbia Race Riots," 180-185; Smedley, *History of the Underground Railroad*, 46.

170. Smedley, *History of the Underground Railroad*, 46.

171. Deborah Wright to Dillwyn Parrish, August 23, November 16, 1835, Parrish Family Papers, Series 2, Swarthmore College; Thomas D. Hamm, "George F. White and Hicksite Opposition to the Abolitionist Movement," in *Quakers and Abolition*, 43–55.

172. Deborah Wright to Dillwyn Parrish, October 29, 1835, Parrish Family Papers, Swarthmore College.

173. Nagle, *Year of Jubilee*, 1:453–56, 485–92.

174. Ibid., 471–83.

175. "Riot," *Pennsylvania Intelligencer*, April 22, 1825.

176. Gerald G. Eggert, "The Impact of the Fugitive Slave Law on Harrisburg: A Case Study," *Pennsylvania Magazine of History and Biography* 109, no. 4 (1985): 541–47; Blackett, *Making Freedom*, 32–35; Blackett, *Captive's Quest for Freedom*, 269–91.

177. Middletown Area Historical Society, "Tribute to the Black Influence," 4–33.

Chapter 7

178. Belles Lettres Society Minutebook, August 12, 1786, November 24, 1787, July 15, 1789, July 26, 1794; Slotten, "McClintock Slave Riot," 18–19, 25.

179. "A Hard Case," *Pennsylvania Freeman*, December 22, 1853; "Agent of the Underground Railway," *Philadelphia Press*, October 15, 1899; Tritt and Watt, *At a Place Called the Boiling Springs*, 111–17.

180. Crooks, *Life and Letters*, 123.

181. Ibid., 124.

182. Ibid., 139.

183. John McClintock Journal, "Riot Documents," Box 7, Folder 6, John McClintock Papers, Stuart A. Rose Library, Emory University.

184. Slotten, "McClintock Slave Riot," 14.

185. Finkelman, "Kidnapping of John Davis," 397–417.

186. Smith, *On the Edge of Freedom*, 19–22.

187. Underground Railroad notes, Jeremiah Zeamer Papers, Cumberland County Historical Society.

188. McClintock Journal, "Riot Documents," Box 7, Folder 6, McClintock Papers, Emory University; Slotten, "McClintock Slave Riot," 14–18.

189. "The Slave Riot at Carlisle, Pa.," newspaper clippings, McClintock drop file, Dickinson College.

190. McClintock Journal, "Riot Documents," Box 7, Folder 6, McClintock Papers, Emory University; Slotten, "McClintock Slave Riot," 17–18.

191. Crooks, *Life and Letters*, 158.

192. Ibid.; Conway, *Autobiography*, 1:51–52.

193. "The Riot at Carlisle: A Card," newspaper clippings, McClintock drop file, Dickinson College.

194. Crooks, *Life and Letters*, 158–77.

195. Robert Emory to George Fechtig, June 7, 1847, Methodist Historical Society, Baltimore (copy at Dickinson College Archives and Special Collections, John McClintock drop file).

196. Emory to Fechtig, June 9, 1847, Methodist Historical Society, Baltimore (copy at McClintock drop file, Dickinson College).

197. Crooks, *Life and Letters*, 158–77.

198. Ibid., 158–79; Slotten, "McClintock Slave Riot," 28–32.

199. *Gettysburg Star & Republican Banner*, March 20, 1837; Blanchard, "Personal Recollections," *Christian Cynosure*, December 29, 1868; Blanchard, "Hon. Thaddeus Stevens," *Christian Cynosure*, April 5, 1883;

"From the Gettysburg Anti-Masonic Star," *Franklin Repository*, newspaper clippings, Underground Railroad file, Franklin County Historical Society. Blanchard's letter to Middleton is dated August 9, 1837.

200. Appel, *Recollections of College Life*, 60–64.

201. Anonymous correspondent to Robert Emory, September 23, 1842, RG 2/2 Presidential Papers, Series 1, Box 1, Dickinson College Archives & Special Collections.

202. Tuscarora Academy Broadside; "Interesting Historical Sketch of Tuscarora Academy," *Juanita Tribune*, September 11, September 19, September 26, 1929.

203. Hamilton and Cameron, *Papers of Randolph Abbott Shotwell*, 1:9–12; "Interesting Historical Sketch of Tuscarora Academy," *Juanita Tribune*, September 26, 1929.

204. Hamilton and Cameron, *Papers of Randolph Abbott Shotwell*, 1:13–20.

205. "Tells of Capturing Roommate at Spottsylvania [*sic*]," *Dickinson Alumnus*, September 1933, 11:1, 18–19.

206. "Agent of the Underground Railway," *Philadelphia Press*, October 15, 1899; Bobb, "Underground Railroad," 1:1–4.

207. Bobb, "Underground Railroad," 1:1–4.

Chapter 8

208. J. Howard Wert, "Recollections of the Underground Railroad," *Harrisburg Telegraph*, December 2, 1904; Switala, *Underground Railroad in Delaware*, 98. The identity of Dr. Chaplin, as the connecting agent from Washington to Gettysburg, is confirmed by the letter of S.R. McAllister to J. Howard Wert, December 2, 1904, J. Howard Wert Gettysburg Collection.

209. J. Howard Wert, "Recollections of the Underground Railroad," *Harrisburg Telegraph*, December 2, 1904.

210. Interview with Theodore McAllister, March 15, 1912, in Gettysburg newspaper clippings, Vol. 6, Gettysburg National Military Park Library.

211. Smedley, *History of the Underground Railroad*, 42–44.

212. *Harrisburg Morning Herald*, June 15, 1854; "The Underground Railroad," *Harrisburg Telegraph*, October 31, 1859; *Harrisburg Telegraph*, November 14, 1859.

213. Marsh, *Bake-Pan*, 45.

214. Wayland, *Dr. Wayland, on the Moral and Religious Aspect*, 2.

215. Baines, *American Slavery*, 7.

Chapter 9

216. Reynolds, *John Brown*, 19–24, 65.

217. Ibid., 138–73, 198–203.

218. Ibid., 239, 248–61.

219. Ibid., 297; Emma Ritner Robert, "Recollections of John Brown," Ritner file, Franklin County Historical Society; "High Treason!" *Franklin Repository*, August 24, 1859; Douglass, *Life and Times of Frederick Douglass*, 387–88; "John Brown and His Men: Inmates of the Ritner Boarding House," *Chambersburg Public Opinion*, February 13, 1891; "He Knew John Brown," *Franklin Repository*, June 9, 1896; Jim Neitzel, "John Brown's Summer of Discontent," in Alexander, *Southern Revenge!*, 11–21; DuBois, *John Brown*, 291–92; Geffert, "John Brown and His Black Allies," 598–99.

220. Douglass, *Life and Times of Frederick Douglass*, 388–91; Geffert, "John Brown and His Black Allies," 598–99.

221. "Owen Brown's Escape from Harper's Ferry," *Atlantic Monthly* 33, no. 197 (March 1874): 342–65; A.K. McClure to J. Howard Wert, [1904], J. Howard Wert Gettysburg Collection.

222. McClure, "Episode of John Brown's Raid," 279–87.

223. "Insurrection at Harper's Ferry," *Valley Spirit*, October 26, 1859; Emma Ritner Robert, "Recollections of John Brown," Ritner File, Franklin County Historical Society; Neitzel, "John Brown's Summer of Discontent," in Alexander, *Southern Revenge!*, 19–21.

224. Anderson, *Voice from Harper's Ferry*, 53–55.

225. Clarke, *Causes and Consequences of the Affair at Harper's Ferry*, 8.

226. Wheelock, *Harper's Ferry and Its Lesson*, 3–4.

227. Douglass, *Life and Times of Frederick Douglass*, 392; Reynolds, *John Brown*, 341–42.

228. Emma Ritner Robert, "Recollections of John Brown," Ritner File, Franklin County Historical Society.

229. "Insurrection at Harper's Ferry," *Valley Spirit*, October 26, 1859.

230. "The Day of Execution," *Franklin Repository*, November 30, 1859.

231. Ibid.

232. "A Few Facts for the Merchants and Manufacturers of the North," *Valley Spirit*, January 25, 1860.

233. "Save Us from Abolitionism," *Valley Spirit*, October 31, 1860.

Epilogue

234. "The Union Safe!" handbill, c. November 1860, J. Howard Wert Gettysburg Collection.

235. *Declaration of the Immediate Causes*, 7–9.

236. *Address Setting forth the Declaration of the Immediate Causes*, 3.

237. "The Union Dissolved," *Valley Spirit*, December 26, 1860.

238. "Circular," April 24, 1861, Herman Merrills Johnson Papers, Dickinson College.

239. "Tells of Capturing Roommate at Spottsylvania [*sic*]," *Dickinson Alumnus* 11, no. 1 (September 1933): 18–19.

240. "Portrait of the Past: Dickinsonians Remembered," *Dickinson Magazine* 6, no. 3 (Summer 1996): 17.

241. Abraham Essick Diary, April 30, May 8, 1861, Franklin County Historical Society.

242. "Tells of Capturing Roommate at Spottsylvania [*sic*]," *Dickinson Alumnus*, 18–19.

243. Herman Merrills Johnson to Abraham Lincoln, c. 1861. Draft of letter proposing colonization of the South, Herman Merrills Johnson Papers, Dickinson College.

244. Interview with Theodore McAllister, March 15, 1912, in Gettysburg newspaper clippings, vol. 6, Gettysburg National Military Park Library.

245. Commission to recruit United States Colored Troops, June 1863, J. Howard Wert Gettysburg Collection.

246. Warner, *Generals in Blue*, 99.

247. William Robinson Diary, *Civil War Times Illustrated* Collection, U.S. Army Heritage and Education Center, Carlisle, PA.

248. W.P. Snakenberg Memoir, typescript at 14th Louisiana Infantry Vertical File, Gettysburg National Military Park Library.

249. Unidentified correspondent, Dickinson Township, PA, to Sidney Boden, July 11, 1863, MS 605, Burgett-Irey Family Papers, Special Collections and University Archives, University of Massachusetts Amherst Libraries, Amherst, MA.

250. Blair, reminisce, Box 120-13, Cumberland County Historical Society, Carlisle, PA.

251. Charles Hartman Diary, June 22, 1863, Schaff Library, Lancaster Theological Seminary.

252. Basil Biggs Petition, Civilian Claims Files, Gettysburg National Military Park Library; Vermilyea, "Effect of Lee's Invasion."

253. Interview with Ida Mary Lewis, in Ruffin, *This Is My Story*, 408–9.
254. McCauslin, *Yellow Hill*, 14–15.
255. Douglass, *Life and Times of Frederick Douglass*, 415–16.
256. "John McClintock, D.D.," *Harper's Weekly*, March 19, 1870.
257. "Laus Deo!" clipping, Lydia Hamilton Smith Papers, J. Howard Wert Gettysburg Collection.
258. Douglass, *Life and Times of Frederick Douglass*, 392.
259. Interview with Theodore McAllister, March 15, 1912, in Gettysburg newspaper clippings, vol. 6, Gettysburg National Military Park Library.

BIBLIOGRAPHY

Books and Articles

An Address Setting Forth the Declaration of the Immediate Causes which Induce and Justify the Secession of Mississippi from the Federal Union and the Ordinance of Secession. Jackson: Mississippian Book and Job Printing Office, 1861.

Adeleke, Tunde. *Without Regard to Race: The Other Martin Robinson Delany.* Jackson: University Press of Mississippi, 2003.

Alexander, Ted. *Southern Revenge! Civil War History of Chambersburg, Pennsylvania.* Shippensburg, PA: White Mane Books, 1989; reprint, 2013.

American Convention for Promoting the Abolition of Slavery. *Minutes of the Adjourned Session of the Twentieth Biennial American Convention for Promoting the Abolition of Slavery, and Improving the Condition of the African Race, Held at Baltimore, Nov. 1828.* Philadelphia: Samuel Parker, 1828.

Anadolu-Okur, Nilgün. *Dismantling Slavery: Frederick Douglas, William Lloyd Garrison, and Formation of the Abolitionist Discourse, 1841–1851.* Knoxville: University of Tennessee Press, 2016.

Anderson, Matthew. *Presbyterianism: Its Relation to the Negro.* Philadelphia: John McGill White & Co., 1897.

Anderson, Osborne P. *A Voice from Harper's Ferry: A Narrative of Events at Harper's Ferry; with Incidents Prior and Subsequent to Its Capture by Captain Brown and His Men.* Boston: for the author, 1861.

Appel, Theodore. *Recollections of College Life, at Marshall College, Mercersburg, Pa., from 1839 to 1845.* Reading, PA: Daniel Miller, 1886.

Armstrong, William Clinton. *The Lundy Family and Their Descendants of Whatsoever Surname, with a Biographical Sketch of Benjamin Lundy.* New Brunswick, NJ: J. Heidingsfeld, 1902.

[Austin, James Trecothick]. *Remarks on Dr. Channing's Slavery.* Boston: Russell, Shattuck and Company, and John H. Eastburn, 1835.

Baines, Edward. *American Slavery: Letter of Edward Baines, Esq.* Leeds, UK: Leeds Anti-Slavery Association, 1854.

Bates, Samuel P., and J. Fraise Richard, eds. *History of Franklin County, Pennsylvania.* Chicago: Warner, Beers & Co., 1887.

Bigelow, Ann Clymer. "Antebellum Ohio's Black Barbers in the Political Vanguard." *Ohio Valley History* 11, no. 2 (Summer 2011).

Blackett, Richard. *The Captive's Quest for Freedom: Fugitive Slaves, the 1850 Fugitive Slave Law, and the Politics of Slavery.* New York: Cambridge University Press, 2018.

———. *Making Freedom: The Underground Railroad and the Politics of Slavery.* Chapel Hill: University of North Carolina Press, 2013.

Brown, Ira V. "Miller McKim and Pennsylvania Abolitionism." *Pennsylvania History* 30 (January 1963).

Cazenove, Theophile. *Cazenove Journal 1794: A Record of the Journey of Theophile Cazenove through New Journey and Pennsylvania.* Edited by Rayner Wickersham Kelsey. Haverford: Pennsylvania History Press, 1922.

Churchman, John. *An Account of the Gospel Labours, and Christian Experiences of a Faithful Minister of Christ, John Churchman.* Philadelphia: Joseph Crukshank, 1779.

Clarke, James Freeman. *Causes and Consequences of the Affair at Harper's Ferry: A Sermon Preached in the Indiana Place Chapel, on Sunday Morning, Nov. 6, 1859.* Boston: Walker, Wise, & Co., 1859.

Clarkson, Thomas. *History of the Rise, Progress, and Accomplishment of the Abolition of the African Slave Trade by the British Parliament.* London: John W. Parker, 1839.

Coffin, Levi. *Reminiscences of Levi Coffin, the Reputed President of the Underground Railroad.* Cincinnati, OH: Robert Clarke & Co., 1880.

Conscience versus Cotton; or, the Preference of Free-Labor-Produce. N.p., n.d. Samuel J. May Anti-Slavery Collection, available online via Cornell University.

Conway, Moncure Daniel. *Autobiography: Memories and Experiences of Moncure Daniel Conway.* Boston: Houghton, Mifflin and Company, 1904.

Crooks, George R. *Life and Letters of the Rev. John McClintock, D.D., LL.D., Late President of Drew Theological Seminary.* New York: Nelson & Phillips, 1876.

Declaration of the Immediate Causes which Induce and Justify the Secession of South Carolina from the Federal Union; and the Ordinance of Secession. Charleston, SC: Evans & Cogswell, 1860.

Dickens, Charles. *American Notes for General Circulation.* London: Chapman and Hall, 1842.

Dillon, Merton L. *Benjamin Lundy and the Struggle for Negro Freedom.* Urbana: University of Illinois Press, 1966.

Douglass, Frederick. *Life and Times of Frederick Douglass, Written by Himself.* Hartford, CT: Park Publishing, 1882.

Drew, Benjamin. *The North-Side View of Slavery; The Refugee: or the Narratives of Fugitive Slaves in Canada.* Boston: John P. Jewett, 1856.

DuBois, W.E.B. *John Brown.* Philadelphia: George W. Jacobs & Company, 1909.

Earle, Thomas, ed. *The Life, Travels, and Opinions of Benjamin Lundy, Including His Journeys to Texas and Mexico, with a Sketch of Contemporary Events, and a Notice of the Revolution on Hayti.* Philadelphia: W.D. Parrish, 1847.

Egerton, Douglas R. *The Wars of Reconstruction: The Brief, Violent History of America's Most Progressive Era.* New York: Bloomsbury Press, 2014.

Eggert, Gerald G. "The Impact of the Fugitive Slave Law on Harrisburg: A Case Study." *Pennsylvania Magazine of History and Biography* 109, no. 4 (1985).

Fifth Annual Report of the Board of Managers of the Massachusetts Anti-Slavery Society, with Some Account of the Annual Meeting, January 25, 1837. Boston: Isaac Knapp, 1837.

Finkelman, Paul. "The Kidnapping of John Davis and the Adoption of the Fugitive Slave Law of 1793." *Journal of Southern History* 56, no. 3 (August 1990).

Foner, Philip S., ed. *Frederick Douglass: Selected Speeches and Writings.* Abridged by Yuval Taylor. Chicago: Lawrence Hill Books, 1999.

[Fox, George]. *Gospel Family Order, Being a Short Discourse Concerning the Ordering of Families, Both of Whites, Blacks and Indians.* N.p., 1676.

Freeman, Donald C., John B. Pickard and Roland H. Woodwell. *Whittier and Whittierland: Portrait of a Poet and His World.* North Andover, MA: Trustees of John Greenleaf Whittier Homestead, 1976.

Garrison, Wendell Phillips, and Francis Jackson Garrison. *William Lloyd Garrison 1805–1879: The Story of His Life Told by His Children.* New York: Century Company, 1885.

Geffert, Hannah N. "John Brown and His Black Allies: An Ignored Alliance." *Pennsylvania Magazine of History and Biography* 126, no. 4 (October 2002).

Gummere, Amelia Mott, ed. *The Journal and Essays of John Woolman.* New York: MacMillan Company, 1922.

Hamilton, J.G. DeRoulhac, and Rebecca Cameron, eds. *The Papers of Randolph Abbott Shotwell.* Raleigh: North Carolina Historical Commission, 1929.

Hamm, Thomas D. "George F. White and Hicksite Opposition to the Abolitionist Movement." In *Quakers and Abolition.* Edited by Brycchan Carey and Geoffrey Plank. Urbana: University of Illinois Press, 2014.

Harrold, Stanley. *Subversives: Antislavery Community in Washington, D.C., 1828–1865.* Baton Rouge: Louisiana State University Press, 2003.

Hoch, Bradley R. *Thaddeus Stevens in Gettysburg: The Making of an Abolitionist.* Gettysburg, PA: Adams County Historical Society, 2005.

Howe, Henry. *Historical Collections of Virginia; Containing a Collection of the Most Interesting Facts, Traditions, Biographical Sketches, Anecdotes, &c.* Charleston, SC: Babcock & Co., 1845.

Hundley, David R. *Social Relations in Our Southern States.* New York: Henry B. Price, 1860.

Jefferson, Thomas. *Notes on the State of Virginia.* Repr., Boston: Wells and Lilly, 1829.

Kaplan, Fred. *John Quincy Adams: American Visionary.* New York: HarperCollins, 2014.

Kittochtinny Historical Society. *The Kittochtinny Historical Society: Papers Read before the Society from March 1903 to February 1905.* Vol. 3. Chambersburg, PA: Repository Printing House, 1906.

Lay, Benjamin. *All Slave-Keepers: That Keep the Innocent in Bondage, APOSTATES.* Philadelphia: for the author, 1737.

Levine, Robert S. *Martin Delany, Frederick Douglass, and the Politics of Representative Identity.* Chapel Hill: University of North Carolina Press, 1997.

[Lundy, Benjamin]. *The War in Texas: A Review of the Facts and Circumstances....* Philadelphia: Merrihew and Gunn, 1836.

Marsh, Leonard. *A Bake-Pan, for the Dough-Faces.* Burlington, VT: C. Goodrich, 1854.

Martineau, Harriet. *Retrospect of Western Travel.* London: Saunders and Otley, 1838.

May, Samuel. *Some Recollections of Our Antislavery Conflict.* Boston: Fields, Osgood, 1869.

McCauslin, Debra Sandoe. *Yellow Hill: Reconstructing the Past Puzzle of a Lost Community.* Gettysburg, PA: For the Cause Productions, 2007.

McClure, Alexander K. "An Episode of John Brown's Raid." *Lippincott's Magazine of Popular Literature and Science* 32 (September 1883).

McKim, James Miller. *A Sketch of the Slave Trade in the District of Columbia, Contained in Two Letters.* Pittsburgh: Pittsburgh and Allegheny Anti-Slavery Society, 1838.

McPherson, Edward. *The Disunion Conspiracy: Speech of Edward McPherson, of PA., Delivered in the House of Representatives, January 23, 1861.* Washington, D.C.: McGill & Witherow, 1861.

Memorial Addresses on the Life and Character of Thaddeus Stevens, Delivered in the House of Representatives, Washington, D.C., December 17, 1868. Washington, D.C.: Government Printing Office, 1869.

Middletown Area Historical Society. "A Tribute to the Black Influence of Middletown." *2010 Middletown Fair.*

Mingus, Scott, Sr. *The Ground Swallowed Them Up: Slavery and the Underground Railroad in York County, Pa.* York, PA: York County History Center, 2016.

Moore, Glover. *The Missouri Controversy 1819–1821.* Repr., Gloucester, MA: University of Kentucky Press, 1953.

Nagle, George F. *The Year of Jubilee: Men of God.* 2 vols. Harrisburg, PA: George F. Nagle, 2010.

Nash, Gary B., and Jean Soderlund. *Freedom by Degrees: Emancipation in Pennsylvania and Its Aftermath.* New York: Oxford University Press, 1991.

Newman, Richard S. *The Transformation of American Abolitionism: Fighting Slavery in the Early Republic.* Chapel Hill: University of North Carolina Press, 2002.

Palmer, Beverly Wilson, and Holly Byers Ochoa. *The Selected Papers of Thaddeus Stevens.* 2 vols. Pittsburgh: University of Pittsburgh Press, 1997.

Phillips, Ulric B. *American Negro Slavery: A Survey of the Supply, Employment and Control of Negro Labor as Determined by the Plantation Regime.* New York: D. Appleton, 1918.

———. *Life and Labor in the Old South.* Boston: Little, Brown and Company, 1929.

Proceedings of the American Anti-Slavery Society, at Its Third Decade, Held in the City of Philadelphia, Dec. 3d and 4th 1863. New York: American Anti-Slavery Society, 1864.

Proceedings of the New England Anti-Slavery Convention: Held in Boston, May 24, 25, 26, 1836. Boston: Isaac Knapp, 1836.

Proceedings of the N.H. Anti-Slavery Convention, Held in Concord, on the 11th and 12th of November, 1834. Concord, NH: Eastman, Webster & Co., 1834.

Proceedings of the Ohio Anti-Slavery Convention, Held at Putnam, on the Twenty-Second, Twenty-Third, and Twenty-Fourth of April 1835. Putnam, OH: Beaumont and Wallace, 1835.

Proceedings of the Pennsylvania Convention, Assembled to Organize a State Anti-Slavery Society, at Harrisburg, On the 31st of January and 1st, 2d and 3d of February 1837. Philadelphia: Merrihew and Gun, 1837.

Proceedings of the Rhode Island Anti-Slavery Convention, Held in Providence, on the 2d, 3d and 4th of February, 1836. Providence, RI: H.H. Brown, 1836.

Prowell, George R. *History of York County, Pennsylvania.* Chicago: J.H. Beers & Co., 1907.

Remini, Robert V. *Andrew Jackson and the Course of American Freedom, 1822–1832.* New York: Harper & Row, 1981.

Reynolds, David S. *John Brown, Abolitionist: The Man Who Killed Slavery, Sparked the Civil War, and Seeded Civil Rights.* New York: Alfred A. Knopf, 2005.

Rohrbough, Malcolm J. *The Land Office Business: The Settlement and Administration of American Public Lands, 1789–1837.* New York: Oxford University Press, 1968.

Ruffin, C. Bernard. *This Is My Story.* Chambersburg, PA, 2003.

Sassi, Jonathan D. "With a Little Help from the Friends: The Quaker and Tactical Contexts of Anthony Benezet's Abolitionist Publishing." *Pennsylvania Magazine of History and Biography* 135, no. 1 (January 2011).

Seilhamer, G.O. *The Bard Family: A History and Genealogy of the Bards of "Carroll's Delight" Together with a Chronicle of the Bards and Genealogies of the Bard Kinship.* Chambersburg, PA: Kittochtinny Press, 1908.

————. *Biographical Annals of Franklin County, Pennsylvania: Containing Genealogical Records of Representative Families, Including Many of the Early settlers, and Biographical Sketches of Prominent Citizens.* Chicago: Genealogical Publishing Company, 1905.

Seward, Frederick W., ed. *William H. Seward: An Autobiography from 1801 to 1834, With a Memoir of His Life, and Selections from His Letters 1831–1846.* New York: D. Appleton and Company, 1877.

Sharpe, J. McDowell. *A Memoir of George Chambers, of Chambersburg, Late Vice-President of the Historical Society of Pennsylvania.* Philadelphia: Historical Society of Pennsylvania, 1873.

Sinha, Manisha. *The Slave's Cause: A History of Abolition.* New Haven, CT: Yale University Press, 2016.

Slotten, Martha C. "The McClintock Slave Riot of 1847." *Cumberland County History* 17, no. 1 (Summer 2000).

Smedley, Robert C. *History of the Underground Railroad in Chester and Neighboring Counties.* Lancaster, PA: John A. Hiestand, 1883.

Smith, David. *On the Edge of Freedom: The Fugitive Slave Issue in South Central Pennsylvania, 1820–1870.* New York: Fordham University Press, 2012.

Soderlund, Jean, and Nicholas Wood. "Notes and Documents: 'To Friends and All Whom It May Concerne': William Southeby's Rediscovered 1696 Antislavery Protest." *Pennsylvania Magazine of History and Biography* 141, no. 2 (April 2017).

Sproull, J.W., and D.B. Willson, eds. *The Reformed Presbyterian and Convenanter.* Vol. 14. N.p., 1876.

Switala, William J. *Underground Railroad in Delaware, Maryland, and West Virginia.* Mechanicsburg, PA: Stackpole Books, 2004.

Third Annual Report of the American Anti-Slavery Society; With the Speeches Delivered at the Anniversary Meeting, Held in the City of New-York, on the 10th May, 1836. New York: William S. Dorr, 1836.

Trefousse, Hans L. *Thaddeus Stevens: Nineteenth-Century Egalitarian.* Chapel Hill: University of North Carolina Press, 1997.

Tritt, Richard L., and Randy Watt, eds. *At a Place Called the Boiling Springs.* N.p.: Boiling Springs Sesquicentennial Publications Committee, 1995.

Turner, Frederick Jackson. *The United States 1830–1850; the Nation and Its Sections.* New York: Peter Smith, 1950.

Vermilyea, Peter C. "The Effect of Lee's Invasion on Gettysburg's African-American Community." *Gettysburg Magazine* (January 2001).

Warner, Beers and Co. *History of Cumberland and Adams Counties, Pennsylvania.* Chicago: Warner, Beers and Co., 1886.

Warner, Ezra J., Jr. *Generals in Blue: Lives of the Union Commanders.* Baton Rouge: Louisiana State University Press, 1964.

Wayland, Francis. *Dr. Wayland, on the Moral and Religious Aspect of the Nebraska Bill, Speech at Providence, R.I., March 7.* Rochester, NY: W.N. Sage, 1854.

Wert, J. Howard. *Episodes of Gettysburg and the Underground Railroad.* Edited by G. Craig Caba. Gettysburg, PA: G. Craig Caba, 1998.

Wheelock, Edwin M. *Harper's Ferry and Its Lesson: A Sermon for the Times.* Boston: Published by the Fraternity, 1859.

Wingert, Cooper H. *Slavery and the Underground Railroad in South Central Pennsylvania.* Charleston, SC: The History Press, 2016.

Worner, William Frederic. "The Columbia Race Riots." In *Papers Read before the Lancaster County Historical Society, Friday, October 6, 1922.* Lancaster, PA: Lancaster Historical Society, 1922.

Government Publications

Annals of Congress.

A Biographical Congressional Directory 1774 to 1903. Washington, D.C.: Government Printing Office, 1903.

Bureau of the Census. *Abstract of the Returns of the Fifth Census.* Washington, D.C.: Duff Green, 1832.

————. *Aggregate Amount of Each Description of Persons within the United States of America, and the Territories Thereof, Agreeably to Actual Enumeration Made According to Law, in the Year 1810.* Washington, D.C.: U.S. Treasury Department, 1811.

————. *Census for 1820.* Washington, D.C.: Gales and Seaton, 1821.

Congressional Globe.

DeBow, James D.B. *Statistical View of the United States...Being a Compendium of the Seventh Census.* Washington, D.C.: A.O.P. Nicholson, 1854.

Pennsylvania Archives (1852–1914). 7 Series.

Newspapers and Periodicals

Adams Centinel (Sentinel)
Atlantic Monthly
Carlisle American Volunteer
Chambersburg Public Opinion
Colored American (formerly the *Weekly Advocate*)
Dickinson Alumnus
Dickinson Magazine
Franklin Repository
Freedom's Journal (New York)
The Friend of Man
Gettysburg Compiler
Gettysburg Star & Republican Banner
Gettysburg Star & Sentinel
Harrisburg Morning Herald
Harrisburg Telegraph
Juniata Tribune
Kline's Carlisle Weekly Gazette
Pennsylvania Freeman
Philadelphia Press
Spirit of Liberty
Valley Spirit

Manuscripts

African-American Collection, Manuscript Group 72, Cumberland County Historical Society, Carlisle, PA.

Amateur Photographic Exchange Club No. 38. "Henry-Janitor-Dickinson College Carlisle Penna." Prof. Charles F. Himes. Prints and Photographs Division, Library of Congress.

Belles Lettres Society Minutebook, 1786–1794, Archives and Special Collections, Dickinson College, Carlisle, PA.

Biggs, Basil. Border Claims. Civil Claims File, Gettysburg National Military Park Library, Gettysburg, PA.

Blair, Nettie Jane. Reminisce. Box 120-13, Cumberland County Historical Society, Carlisle, PA.

Bobb, Mary C. "An Underground Railroad." *Lamberton and Hamilton Library Association Prize Essays* 1 (1912): 1–4. Cumberland County Historical Society.

Essick, Abraham. Diary. Franklin County Historical Society, Chambersburg, PA.

Gettysburg Newspaper Clippings. Gettysburg National Military Park Library, Gettysburg, PA.

Hartman, Charles. Diary. Schaff Library, Lancaster Theological Seminary, Lancaster, PA.

Jackson, Andrew. Papers. Library of Congress.

Jackson, Halliday. Letterbook. Friends Historical Library, Swarthmore College, Swarthmore, PA.

Jefferson, Thomas. Papers. Library of Congress.

Johnson, Hermann Merrills. Papers. Archives and Special Collections, Dickinson College, Carlisle, PA.

Lewis, Graceanna. Underground Railroad memoirs. Lewis-Fussell Family Papers, Friends Historic Library, Swarthmore College, Swarthmore, PA.

McClintock, John. Drop file. Archives and Special Collections, Dickinson College, Carlisle, PA.

———. Journal, "Riot Documents." John McClintock Papers, Stuart A. Rose Library, Emory University.

Presidential Papers, RG 2/2. Archives and Special Collections, Dickinson College, Carlisle, PA.

Ritner Family File. Franklin County Historical Society, Chambersburg, PA.

Robinson, William. Diary. Civil War Times Illustrated Collection, U.S. Army Heritage and Education Center, Carlisle, PA.

BIBLIOGRAPHY

Ruffin, C. Bernard. "Slavery, Civil War, and Emancipation." Oral interview transcripts. Franklin County Historical Society, Chambersburg, PA.

Slavery file. York County Heritage Trust, York, PA.

Smith, Lydia Hamilton. "Certificate of Death." February 14, 1884. Vital Records Division, Department of Health, Washington, D.C.

Snakenberg, W.P. Memoir. 14th Louisiana Infantry Vertical File. Gettysburg National Military Park Library, Gettysburg, PA.

Tax Records, Carlisle Borough, 1829–1844. Cumberland County. Transcripts at Cumberland County Historical Society, Carlisle, PA.

Tuscarora Academy Broadside, circa 1850. Palmer Museum of Art, Pennsylvania State University, copy courtesy of the Juanita County Historical Society.

Underground Railroad file. Franklin County Historical Society, Chambersburg, PA.

Underground Railroad file. York County Heritage Trust, York, PA.

Unidentified correspondent, Dickinson Township, PA, to Sidney Boden, July 11, 1863, MS 605. Burgett-Irey Family Papers, Special Collections and University Archives, University of Massachusetts Amherst Libraries, Amherst, MA.

Wert, J. Howard Collection. Private Collection.

Wright, Deborah. Letters to Nephew, 1835. Parrish Family Papers, Series 2. Friends Historic Library, Swarthmore College, Swarthmore, PA.

Zeamer, Jeremiah. Papers. Cumberland County Historical Society, Carlisle, PA.

INDEX

ABOUT THE AUTHOR

Cooper Wingert is the author of ten books, including *The Confederate Approach on Harrisburg* and *Slavery and the Underground Railroad in South Central Pennsylvania*. He is the recipient of the 2012 Dr. James I. Robertson Literary Award for Confederate History. He has been featured on C-SPAN's *Book TV* and Pennsylvania Cable Network. Wingert currently resides in Enola, Pennsylvania.

Visit us at
www.historypress.com